Christmas Celebrations

Christmas
Celebrations

Festive recipes, hand-crafted gifts and decorative
ideas for the yuletide season

LORENZ BOOKS

First published in 1999 by Lorenz Books
© Anness Publishing Limited 1999

Lorenz Books is an imprint of
Anness Publishing Limited, Hermes House, 88–89 Blackfriars Road,
London SE1 8HA

This edition distributed in Canada by Raincoast Books,
8680 Cambie Street, Vancouver, British Columbia V6P 6M9

ISBN 0 7548 0300 7

A CIP catalogue record for this book is available from the British Library

Publisher: Joanna Lorenz
Project editor: Simona Hill
Designer: Jonathan Harley
Illustrators: Anna Koska, Nadine Wickenden, Lorraine Harrison
Production controller: Wendy Lawson

Printed and bound in Singapore

3 5 7 9 10 8 6 4 2

ACKNOWLEDGEMENTS
The publishers would like to thank the following craftspeople: Fiona Barnett, Petra Boase, Penny Boylan, Louise Brownlow, Lynda Burgess,
Carole Clements, Annabel Crutchley, Roz Denny, Stephanie Donaldson, Marion Elliot, Tessa Evelegh, Joanna Farrow, Stephanie Harvey,
Christine Kingdom, Gilly Love, Sue Maggs, Mary Maguire, Terence Moore, Janice Murfitt, Gloria Nichol, Cheryl Owen, Theresa Pateman,
Katherine Richmond, Deborah Schneebeli-Morrell, Andrea Spencer, Isabel Stanley, Liz Trigg, Liz Wagstaff, Stewart and Sally Walton,
Pamela Westland, Emma Whitfield, Elizabeth Wolf-Cohen, Dorothy Wood, Ann Zwemmer.

Thanks also to the following photographers: Karl Adamson, Edward Allright, Steve Dalton, James Duncan, John Freeman, Michelle Garrett,
Nelson Hargreaves, Amanda Heywood, Janine Hosegood, Tim Imrie, Gloria Nicol, Debbie Patterson, Graham Rae, Heine Schneebeli,
Steve Tanner, Peter Williams, Polly Wreford.

CONTENTS

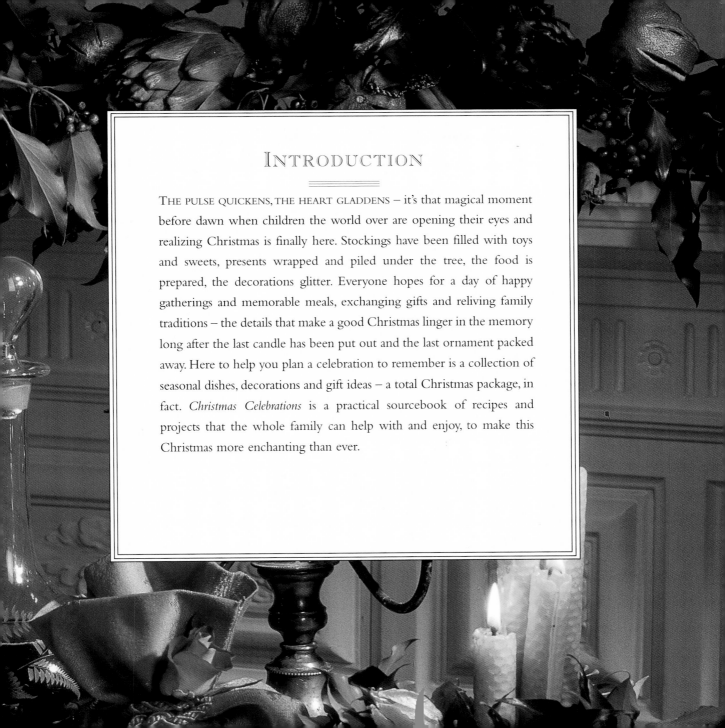

INTRODUCTION

THE PULSE QUICKENS, THE HEART GLADDENS – it's that magical moment before dawn when children the world over are opening their eyes and realizing Christmas is finally here. Stockings have been filled with toys and sweets, presents wrapped and piled under the tree, the food is prepared, the decorations glitter. Everyone hopes for a day of happy gatherings and memorable meals, exchanging gifts and reliving family traditions – the details that make a good Christmas linger in the memory long after the last candle has been put out and the last ornament packed away. Here to help you plan a celebration to remember is a collection of seasonal dishes, decorations and gift ideas – a total Christmas package, in fact. *Christmas Celebrations* is a practical sourcebook of recipes and projects that the whole family can help with and enjoy, to make this Christmas more enchanting than ever.

FESTIVE FOOD

A COLLECTION OF TRADITIONAL SEASONAL
FAVOURITES, TOGETHER WITH SOME MODERN
FLOURISHES, TO DELIGHT THE PALATE.

$\mathscr{C}$OCKTAILS

CHAMPAGNE COCKTAILS AND SPARKLING PUNCHES have just what it takes to welcome Christmas guests.
A bracing alcohol-free Cranberry Frost is an ebullient accompaniment to a late breakfast or leisurely brunch.
When the main meal is to be served in the evening, the more spirited Kir Royale has the sparkle to set the
scene, as the family – or at least the adult members of it – gets into the swing of the Christmas festivities.

CRANBERRY FROST

Makes 10 servings

INGREDIENTS
*115g/4oz/½ cup caster
  (superfine) sugar
juice of 2 oranges
120ml/4fl oz/½ cup
  cranberry juice
1.2 litres/2 pints/5 cups
  chilled soda water
cranberries and fresh mint to
  garnish*

1 Combine the sugar,
orange juice and 120ml/
4fl oz/½ cup of water in a
small saucepan over a low
heat and stir until the
sugar is dissolved. Bring to
the boil, boiling for
3 minutes. Allow to cool.
(The syrup can be made
in advance and stored in
the refrigerator.)

2 Place the syrup in a
chilled punch bowl, add
the cranberry juice and
mix well. Just before
serving, add the soda water
and garnish with cranber-
ries and mint sprigs.

KIR ROYALE

Makes 1 serving

INGREDIENTS
*30ml/2 tbsp crème de cassis
120ml/4fl oz/½ cup
  champagne
orange slice, to garnish*

Place the crème de cassis in
a chilled champagne flute.
Add the champagne and
stir to combine. Garnish
with an orange slice.

ICE FOLLIES

Add flair to cocktails and
punches with stylish ice
cubes. For coloured ice, stir

a few drops of food
colouring into the water
before freezing it in ice-
cube trays, then harmonize
the colours of the ice and
the cocktails.

Freeze strawberries,
raspberries, blackberries or
melon balls in ice-cube

trays. Place the fruit in each
section and then fill it up
with water. Try freezing
small (non-toxic!) flowers
or herbs in a similar way.

*Stylish ice cubes make pretty
drinks (above). Cranberry Frost
(opposite) is a bracing punch.*

Appetizers

Balance is the key when planning dips, pâtés and snacks to serve with drinks. Whether you're preparing appetizers or a buffet for a cocktail party, make your selections as varied as possible. Quick dips and marinated vegetables are a good starting point.

SMOKED TROUT PÂTÉ

Makes 2 servings

INGREDIENTS

115g/4oz/½ cup ricotta cheese
120ml/4fl oz/½ cup soured (sour) cream
115g/4oz/1 cup smoked trout fillets, flaked
30ml/2 tbsp creamed (prepared) horseradish
3 spring onions (scallions)
15ml/1 tbsp dill or parsley
10ml/2 tsp lemon juice
salt and black pepper
trimmed radishes, black bread (pumpernickle), and onion slices, to serve

1 Combine the ricotta and soured (sour) cream in a food processor and purée. Transfer to a bowl.

2 Fold in the trout, horseradish, chopped spring onions (scallions), chopped dill or parsley, lemon juice and salt and pepper. Transfer the pâté to a serving bowl and chill.

3 Serve with radishes, black bread (pumpernickle) and onion slices.

MARINATED CARROTS

Makes 8 servings

INGREDIENTS

450g/1lb carrots, thinly sliced
250ml/8fl oz/1 cup fresh orange juice
15ml/1 tbsp sugar
tarragon or mint leaves

Combine all the ingredients in a bowl and marinate overnight. Drain and serve.

HERBED STILTON

Makes 8 servings

INGREDIENTS

225g/8oz Stilton or other blue cheese
115g/4oz/½ cup cream cheese
15ml/1 tbsp port
15ml/1 tbsp chopped parsley
15ml/1 tbsp chopped chives
50g/2oz/½ cup finely chopped walnuts, lightly toasted
salt and freshly ground black pepper

1 Place the Stilton or other blue cheese, cream cheese and port in a food processor. Blend until smooth.

2 Transfer to a mixing bowl and stir in the remaining ingredients.

3 Spoon into ramekins, chill and serve.

Crudités and vegetable garnishes embellish pâtés such as Herbed Stilton and Smoked Trout.

HOT ARTICHOKE PASTRY PUFFS

Makes 24 servings

INGREDIENTS
FOR THE FILLING

25g/1oz/2 tbsp unsalted (sweet) butter
65g/2½oz/9 tbsp flour
150ml/¼ pint/⅔ cup single (light) cream
30ml/2 tbsp milk
generous pinch of cayenne
225g/8oz can artichoke hearts, finely chopped
salt and black pepper

FOR THE PASTRY

450g/1lb frozen puff pastry, thawed
1 egg, beaten, for glazing

1 Melt the butter in a saucepan over a medium heat. Stir in the flour and cook for 5 minutes. Stir in the cream and milk and season with salt, pepper and cayenne. Bring to a gentle boil and simmer, stirring constantly, for

---

TIP

For extra flavour use anchovy- or almond-stuffed olives to make Cheese and Olive Bites.

3 minutes. Remove from the heat. Stir in the artichoke hearts and cool to room temperature.

2 Preheat the oven to 200°C/400°F/Gas 6. Roll out the puff pastry on a floured board to a thickness of about 3mm/⅛in. Using a 7.5cm/3in fluted cookie cutter, cut the pastry into rounds. Brush the rim of each round with beaten egg.

3 Spoon some filling on to a round. Cover with another round, and seal.

4 Brush the pastry tops with egg. Bake on a baking sheet for 18–20 minutes, until golden.

CHEESE AND OLIVE BITES

Serve these delicious bite-size morsels chilled, speared with cocktail sticks (toothpicks).

INGREDIENTS

225g/8oz/1 cup cream cheese, at room temperature
about 16 stuffed green olives
50g/2oz/½ cup chopped .walnuts, lightly toasted

1 In a mixing bowl, beat the cream cheese until soft. Mould generous teaspoonfuls of the cheese around each olive. Roll them between your palms to form neat spheres.

2 Place the chopped walnuts in a saucer. Roll the coated olives in the nuts to cover them evenly. Chill for at least 1 hour before serving.

Hot Artichoke Pastry Puffs are served with cherry tomatoes. Olives are surrounded by choux pastry puffs.

WATERCRESS AND ORANGE SOUP

THIS HEALTHY AND REFRESHING SOUP is equally good served hot or chilled.

Makes 4 servings

INGREDIENTS
15ml / 1 tbsp olive oil
1 large onion, chopped
2 bunches watercress, trimmed
grated rind and juice of
  1 large orange
1 vegetable stock cube
  (bouillon), dissolved in
  600ml / 1 pint / 2½ cups
  boiling water
150ml / ¼ pint / ⅔ cup
  single (light) cream
10ml / 2 tsp cornflour
  (cornstarch)
yogurt, to garnish
4 orange wedges, to serve

TIP
Wash the water-
cress only if really
necessary; it is
often very clean
when purchased.

1 Heat the oil in a large,
non-aluminium saucepan
over a medium heat. Add
the onion and cook until
translucent. Add the watercress, cover and cook for
about 5 minutes, until the
watercress is soft.

2 Add the orange rind,
juice and stock. Cover and
simmer for 15 minutes.
Purée in a food processor.

3 In a bowl, stir together
the single (light) cream and
the cornflour (cornstarch).
Stir into the soup.

4 Return the soup to the
boil over a very low heat,
stirring until just slightly
thickened. Season to taste
with salt and pepper. If
serving chilled, transfer the
soup to a mixing bowl,
cover and refrigerate.

5 Serve the soup with
a swirl of yogurt, and a
wedge of orange to
squeeze into it at the table.

Christmas Salad

A LIGHT FIRST COURSE that can be prepared ahead and assembled just before serving.

Makes 8 servings

INGREDIENTS

FOR THE CARAMELIZED ORANGE PEEL
15ml/1 tbsp caster (superfine) sugar
60ml/4 tbsp cold water
4 oranges

FOR THE SALAD
Mixed salad leaves
2 pink grapefruits
1 large or 2 small avocados, pitted, peeled and cubed

FOR THE DRESSING
90ml/6 tbsp olive oil
30ml/2 tbsp red wine vinegar
1 garlic clove, crushed
1 tsp Dijon mustard
salt and freshly ground black pepper

1 Place the sugar and water in a small saucepan and heat gently until the sugar is dissolved.

2 Remove the rind from the oranges. Scrape away the pith and slice into shreds. Add to the sugar and water, raise the heat and boil for 5 minutes.

3 Drain the rind on a wire rack. Set the syrup aside to cool. You can make the recipe up to this point several days in advance.

4 Tear the salad leaves into pieces and set aside. Peel the grapefruit. Working over a bowl to catch any juice, cut the pith off the grapefruit and the oranges and segment them, removing all the pith and membrane.

5 Place all the dressing ingredients in a jar and shake until emulsified. Add the reserved syrup and adjust the seasoning. Arrange the leaves and fruit on chilled salad plates with the cubed avocados and top with the dressing and the caramelized orange peel.

Shellfish with Seasoned Broth

Leave a few mussels and prawns (shrimps) in their shells to add a flamboyant touch to this elegant dish.

Makes 4 servings

INGREDIENTS
675g/1½lb mussels, scrubbed
and debearded
1 onion, thinly sliced
1 leek, thinly sliced
1 small carrot, julienned
1 garlic clove
1 litre/1¼ pints/4 cups water
pinch of curry powder
pinch of saffron
1 bay leaf
450g/1lb large prawns,
(shrimps) peeled and
deveined
450g/1lb scallops
175g/6oz cooked lobster
meat, sliced (optional)
15–30ml/1–2 tbsp chopped
chervil or parsley
salt and freshly ground
black pepper

1 Place the mussels in a large, heavy soup pot or flameproof casserole and cover the pan tightly. Cook, shaking the pan occasionally, over high heat for 4-6 minutes, until the mussels open. Remove from the heat.

2 When the mussels are cool enough to handle, discard any that have not opened. Remove all but 8 mussels from their shells, reserving a few for presentation, and set aside. Discard the empty shells. Strain the cooking liquid through muslin (cheesecloth) and set aside for later use.

3 Place the onion, leek, carrot and garlic in a large, heavy pot and add the water, reserved cooking liquid, spices and the bay leaf. Bring to the boil, skimming any foam that rises to the surface, then reduce the heat, cover and simmer gently for 20 minutes, until the vegetables are tender. Remove the garlic clove.

4 Add the prawns (shrimps), scallops, and lobster meat, if using. After 1 minute, add the mussels. Simmer gently for about 3 minutes, until the scallops are opaque and all the shellfish is heated through. Adjust the seasoning. Ladle the soup into a heated tureen or shallow soup bowls and sprinkle with herbs.

> **TIP**
> If desired, cook and shell the mussels and simmer the vegetables in the broth ahead of time. Finish the soup just before serving.

Roast Turkey

For the stunning main attraction, serve this golden bird with Brussels sprouts and roast potatoes.

Makes 8 servings

INGREDIENTS
FOR THE STUFFING
225g/8oz lean bacon,
chopped
1 large onion, finely
chopped
450g/1lb pork sausagemeat
(bulk sausage)
25g/1oz/⅓ cup rolled oats
30ml/2 tbsp chopped parsley
10ml/2 tsp mixed dried
herbs
1 large egg, beaten
115g/4oz/½ cup dried
apricots, finely chopped
salt and freshly ground
black pepper

FOR THE TURKEY
1 turkey with giblets (about
4.5kg/10lb, thawed
overnight if frozen)
1 large onion, stuck with
6 whole cloves
50g/2oz/4 tbsp unsalted
(sweet) butter
10 sausages

FOR THE GRAVY
475ml/16fl oz/2 cups
homemade giblet stock or
turkey stock
30ml/2 tbsp flour

1 For the stuffing, sauté the bacon in a medium, heavy frying pan until crisp. Pour off most of the fat, add the onion and sauté gently until the onion is tender and golden brown.

2 Transfer the sautéed bacon and onion to a large mixing bowl and stir in all the remaining stuffing ingredients. Toss well to combine thoroughly. Season well with salt and pepper.

10 To make the gravy, place the giblet stock in a medium saucepan over a medium heat and bring to a simmer.

3 Remove the giblets and neck bone and stuff the neck end of the turkey only. Tuck under the flap of skin and secure with a small skewer. (Do not overstuff the turkey or the skin will burst during roasting.) Reserve any remaining stuffing.

5 Spread the butter over the turkey and season with salt and pepper. Cover loosely with foil and cook for 30 minutes. Baste with the pan juices.

7 While the turkey is cooking, shape the remaining stuffing into small balls or pack it into a greased ovenproof dish.

11 Spoon off the fat from the roasting pan, leaving the meat juices. Blend in the flour and cook over a medium heat for 2 minutes. Gradually stir in the hot stock and bring to the boil. Adjust the seasoning and pour into a gravy boat.

6 Reduce the oven temperature to 180°C/350°F/Gas 4 and cook for 2 hours longer. Baste every 30 minutes. Remove the foil for the last hour of cooking and baste. The turkey is cooked if the juices run clear when the thickest part of the thigh is pierced with a skewer.

8 About 20 minutes before the turkey is done, put the sausages in an ovenproof dish and bake for 20 minutes. Bake the stuffing balls until golden brown and crisp, also about 20 minutes.

9 Transfer the turkey to a platter, cover with foil and let it rest for 15 minutes before carving.

4 Put the clove-studded onion inside the turkey and tie the legs together with twine. Place the turkey in a roasting pan. Adjust the oven racks to allow for the size of the turkey. Preheat the oven to 200°C/400°F/Gas 6.

12 Just before serving, remove the skewer and twine from the roast turkey. Pour any juices that have accumulated while the turkey was resting from the platter into the gravy. To serve, surround the turkey with sausages and stuffing balls. Carve at the table and serve.

VARIATION

An alternative stuffing: in a large bowl, combine fresh breadcrumbs with rendered bacon, sautéed onions and celery. Stir in chopped fresh sage, chopped pitted prunes, toasted hazelnut pieces, melted butter, turkey or chicken stock, salt and a generous grinding of pepper. Bake as directed.

Venison with Cranberry Sauce

Lean and low in fat, venison steaks are a healthy choice for a special occasion. Served with a sauce of fresh, seasonal cranberries, port and ginger, they make a dish with a wonderful combination of flavours. If you wish, substitute pork tenderloin for the venison; it makes an equally festive main course.

Makes 4 servings

INGREDIENTS

1 orange
1 lemon
150g/5oz/1¼ cups fresh
*   or frozen cranberries,*
*   picked over*
5ml/1 tsp grated fresh ginger
1 thyme sprig
5ml/1 tsp Dijon mustard
50ml/2fl oz/¼ cup redcurrant
*   jelly*
150ml/¼ pint/⅔ cup ruby
*   port*
30ml/2 tbsp vegetable oil
4 venison steaks
2 shallots, finely chopped
salt and freshly ground
*   black pepper*
thyme sprigs, to garnish
mashed potatoes, to serve
*   (optional)*
steamed broccoli, to serve
*   (optional)*

1 Pare the rind from half the orange and half the lemon and cut it into very fine strips. Blanch in boiling water for about 5 minutes. Drain the strips and refresh under cold water.

2 Squeeze the orange and lemon and place the juices in a small saucepan. Add the cranberries, grated ginger, thyme sprig, mustard, redcurrant jelly and port.

3 Cook over a medium-low heat until the jelly melts. Bring the mixture to the boil, stirring occasionally, then cover the pan and reduce the heat. Cook gently for about 15 minutes, until the cranberries are just tender.

4 Heat the vegetable oil in a large, heavy frying pan until hot but not smoking. Add the venison steaks and sauté over a high heat for 2–3 minutes. Turn the steaks and add the chopped shallots to the frying pan. Cook 2–3 minutes longer, depending on whether you want to serve the venison rare or medium.

5 Just before the steaks are done, add the cranberry mixture to the frying pan, along with the lemon and orange rind. Bring the mixture to the boil and simmer for a few seconds, until slightly thickened. Remove and discard the thyme sprig. Taste the sauce and adjust the seasoning.

6 Transfer the venison steaks to warmed individual serving plates and spoon some of the cranberry sauce over each serving. Garnish each plate with one or two thyme sprigs and serve immediately with creamy mashed potatoes and steamed broccoli, if desired.

Salmon with Green Peppercorns

The piquancy of green peppercorns perfectly offsets the richness of the pan-fried salmon and smooth, cream sauce in this pretty dish. Be careful not to overcook the fish.

Makes 4 servings

Ingredients

15g/½oz/1 tbsp butter
2 or 3 shallots, finely chopped
15ml/1 tbsp brandy (optional)
50ml/2fl oz/¼ cup dry white wine
90ml/6 tbsp stock
120ml/4fl oz/½ cup double (heavy) cream
30–45ml/2–3 tbsp green peppercorns in brine, rinsed
30–45ml/2–3 tbsp vegetable oil
4 salmon fillets
salt and freshly ground black pepper
fresh parsley, to garnish

1 Melt the butter in a saucepan over a medium heat. Add the shallots and cook for 2 minutes.

2 Add the brandy, if using, the white wine and the stock. Bring to the boil and continue boiling, stirring occasionally.

3 Reduce the heat to medium-low. Add the cream and half the green peppercorns, crushing them slightly.

4 Cook for 4–5 minutes, until the sauce is thickened, then strain and stir in the remaining peppercorns. Keep the sauce warm over a low heat, stirring occasionally, while you cook the salmon.

5 In a heavy frying pan, heat the oil over a medium-high heat until it just starts to smoke. Lightly season the salmon fillets with salt and pepper, place them in the frying pan and cook for 3–4 minutes, until they are opaque throughout. The flesh should flake easily with a fork.

6 To serve, transfer the salmon fillets to warmed plates and top with the sauce. Garnish each serving with a sprig of parsley.

Tip

To make a simple fish stock, place about 450g/1lb bones and trimmings (preferably from a mild, white fish) in a saucepan with a chopped small onion, a chopped carrot and a chopped celery stalk, 6 white peppercorns and 6 whole cloves, a bouquet garni, a little dry white wine and cold water to cover. Simmer for 15 minutes only. If cooked too long the stock will be bitter. Skim and strain.

Lentil and Nut Roast

An excellent celebration dish that can be served with traditional festive trimmings, accompanied by vegetarian gravy. Garnish it with fresh cranberries and parsley sprigs for a really pretty effect.

Makes 6–8 servings

INGREDIENTS
150g/5oz/⅔ cup red lentils
115g/4oz/1 cup hazelnuts
115g/4oz/1 cup walnuts
50g/2oz/4 tbsp butter
1 large carrot, chopped
2 celery stalks, chopped
1 large onion, chopped
115g/4oz mushrooms, chopped
10ml/2 tsp curry powder
30ml/2 tbsp tomato ketchup
30ml/2 tbsp vegetarian
*   Worcestershire sauce*
1 egg, beaten
10ml/2 tsp salt
60ml/4 tbsp chopped parsley
150ml/¼ pint/⅔ cup water
Vegetarian Gravy to serve

1 Soak the lentils for 1 hour in cold water to cover, then drain well. Grind the hazelnuts and walnuts together in a food processor until fine but not a paste. Set aside.

2 Melt the butter in a frying pan. Add the vegetables and sauté over a medium heat for about 5 minutes, until softened. Add the curry powder.

3 Combine the lentils, nuts, vegetables, ketchup, Worcestershire sauce, egg, salt, parsley and water.

4 Grease a loaf tin and line it with greaseproof paper. Press the lentil mixture into the prepared tin and smooth the top.

5 Preheat the oven to 190°C/375°F/Gas 5. Bake the roast for about 1¼ hours, until just firm. Cover with a sheet of aluminium foil.

6 Let the roast rest for 15 minutes before turning it out on to a serving platter and peeling off the paper. Serve immediately with Vegetarian Gravy.

VEGETARIAN GRAVY

Make a large batch and freeze it in containers.

Makes about 1.2 litres/ 2 pints/5 cups

INGREDIENTS
90ml/6 tbsp vegetable oil
1 large red onion, sliced
3 turnips, sliced
3 celery stalks, sliced
115g/4oz/1⅔ cup mush-
*   rooms, trimmed and halved*
2 garlic cloves
1.5 litres/2½ pints/6¼ cups
*   vegetable stock or water*
45ml/3 tbsp soy sauce
salt and black pepper
generous pinch of sugar

1 Heat the oil in a large saucepan over a medium-high heat. Add the onion, turnips, celery, mushrooms and garlic. Cook, stirring occasionally, until well browned – 15–20 minutes.

2 Add the stock or water and soy sauce and bring to the boil. Cover and simmer for another 20 minutes.

3 Purée the vegetables by rubbing them through a sieve with the back of a spoon. Add a little more stock or water to correct the consistency, and return the purée to the pan.

4 Season to taste with salt and pepper. Add the sugar. Freeze at least half the gravy for future use.

Two Vegetable Side Dishes

THESE ENCHANTING VEGETABLE MÉLANGES make excellent accompaniments to meats such as roast turkey.

BRAISED RED CABBAGE WITH APPLE

Makes 6 servings

INGREDIENTS

1 small red cabbage (about
1kg/2¼lb), quartered
and cored
7.5ml/1½ tsp caraway seeds
40g/1½oz/3 tbsp
brown sugar
2 medium red onions, halved
and thinly sliced
2 Red Delicious apples,
peeled, cored, halved and
thinly sliced
45ml/3 tbsp red wine vinegar
25g/1oz/2 tbsp butter, diced
salt and black pepper
chopped parsley, to garnish

1   Preheat the oven to 200°C/400°F/Gas 6.

2   Slice the cabbage quarters thinly.

3   Place one-quarter of the sliced cabbage in the bottom of a flameproof casserole. Season with salt and pepper.

4   Add another layer of the cabbage. Sprinkle with caraway seeds and 15ml/ 1 tbsp of the sugar. Layer one-third of the onions and apples on top.

5   Continue layering until all the ingredients have been used, ending with a layer of sliced cabbage.

6   Pour the red wine vinegar over the cabbage and dot the top with the butter. Cover and bake for 1 hour.

7   Remove the cover and continue baking until the cabbage is very tender and the liquid has evaporated, about 30 minutes longer. Garnish with chopped parsley.

GLAZED CARROTS WITH SPRING ONIONS (SCALLIONS)

Makes 6 servings

INGREDIENTS

450g/1lb baby carrots,
trimmed and peeled
if necessary
40g/1½oz/3 tbsp butter
30ml/2 tbsp honey
30ml/2 tbsp orange juice
225g/8oz spring onions
(scallions), trimmed and cut
diagonally into 2.5cm/1in
lengths
salt and black pepper

1   Cook the carrots in boiling salted water or steam them until just tender, about 10 minutes. Drain if necessary.

2   Melt the butter in a large, heavy frying pan over a low heat. Add the honey and orange juice and cook, stirring, until the mixture is smooth.

3   Add the carrots and spring onions (scallions) and cook over a medium heat, stirring occasionally, until the vegetables are heated through and glazed. Season with salt and pepper before serving.

Garlic Mashed Potatoes

THESE CREAMY, MASHED POTATOES are perfect with all kinds of roasted or sautéed meats – and although it seems like a lot of garlic, the flavour is sweet and subtle when it is cooked this way.

Makes 6-8 servings

INGREDIENTS
2 garlic heads, separated into
cloves, unpeeled
115g/4oz/½ cup butter
1.5kg/3lb baking potatoes
120–175ml/4–6 fl oz/
½–¾ cup milk
salt and white pepper

1 Bring a small saucepan of water to the boil over a high heat. Add the garlic cloves and boil for 2 minutes, then drain and peel each clove with a sharp paring knife.

2 In a heavy frying pan, melt half the butter over a low heat. Add the garlic cloves, cover the pan and cook gently, stirring occasionally, for 20–25 minutes, until very tender and golden. Do not brown the garlic.

3 Cool the garlic and butter slightly and spoon into a food processor; pulse until smooth. Transfer to a bowl, press clear film on to the surface and set aside.

4 Peel and quarter the potatoes, place in a large saucepan and add just enough cold water to cover them. Salt the water generously and bring to the boil over a high heat. Cook until tender.

5 Drain the boiled potatoes in a colander and work through a food mill or ricer, or press through a sieve back into the saucepan.

6 Return to a medium heat and, using a wooden spoon, stir the potatoes for 1 minute to dry them out. Remove from the heat.

7 Warm the milk gently until bubbles form around the edge. Add the remaining butter and stir until melted. Gradually beat the milk, butter and puréed garlic into the potatoes, then season with salt, if needed, and white pepper.

Brussels Sprouts Chataigne

In this dish, Brussels sprouts are braised with chestnuts, which are very popular in the winter months.

Makes 4–6 servings

INGREDIENTS

225g/8oz chestnuts
120ml/4fl oz/½ cup milk
450g/1lb small, tender
*   Brussels sprouts*
25g/1oz/2 tbsp butter
1 shallot, finely chopped
30–45ml/2–3 tbsp dry
*   white wine*

1 Score a cross in the base of each chestnut. Bring a saucepan of water to the boil, add the chestnuts and boil for 6 minutes. Remove a few chestnuts.

2 Holding each chestnut in a paper towel, remove the outer shell with a knife and peel off the inner skin.

3 When all the chestnuts are peeled, discard the cooking water and rinse the pan. Return the peeled chestnuts to the pan and add the milk.

4 Add enough water to cover them completely. Bring to a simmer over a medium heat and cook for 12–15 minutes, until the chestnuts are just tender. Drain and set aside.

5 Remove any wilted or yellow leaves from the Brussels sprouts. Trim the root ends, but leave them intact, or the leaves will separate during cooking. Score a cross in the base of each sprout.

6 In a large, heavy frying pan, melt the butter over a medium heat. Cook the shallot for 1–2 minutes, until just softened.

7 Add the Brussels sprouts and the wine. Cook, covered, over a medium heat for 6–8 minutes, shaking the pan occasionally and adding a little water if necessary.

8 Add the chestnuts. Cover and cook for 3–5 minutes, until the chestnuts and sprouts are tender.

Christmas Pudding

MAKE TRADITIONAL CHRISTMAS PUDDINGS well in advance, wrap them in muslin and store in an airtight container for up to a year to allow the flavours to develop. Make several to give as gifts to friends and relatives.

Makes 6 servings

INGREDIENTS

115g/4oz/1 cup plain (all-purpose) flour
pinch of salt
5ml/1 tsp ground allspice
2.5ml/½ tsp ground cinnamon
1.5ml/¼ tsp grated nutmeg
225g/8oz/1 cup white vegetable fat (crisco), frozen and finely grated
1 apple, grated
115g/4oz/2 cups fresh white breadcrumbs
375g/13oz/2 cups brown sugar
50g/2oz slivered almonds
375g/13oz/1¾ cups raisins
375g/13oz/1½ cups currants
375g/13oz/1½ cups sultanas (golden raisins)
115g/4oz/dried apricots
115g/4oz/¼ cup chopped mixed candied citrus peel
rind and juice of 1 lemon
30ml/2 tbsp treacle (molasses)
3 large eggs
300ml/½ pint/1¼ cups milk
30ml/2 tbsp dark rum
fresh holly sprigs, to garnish

1 Sift together the flour, salt and spices into a large bowl. Stir in the grated vegetable fat (crisco), apple and other dry ingredients, including the grated lemon rind.

2 Heat the treacle (molasses) until runny. Pour onto dry ingredients.

3 In a separate bowl, combine the eggs, milk, rum and lemon juice and stir into the dry mixture.

4 Spoon the mixture into two medium-size pudding bowls or moulds. If using bowls, cover the puddings with greaseproof (waxed) paper, pleating the paper to allow for expansion, and tie with string. If using moulds, fill about two-thirds full.

5 Steam each pudding on a trivet in a large pan of boiling water for 10 hours. Replenish the water frequently (use boiling water) to keep the pans from boiling dry. Cool and store.

6 When ready to serve the pudding, steam for 3 hours. Cool slightly and turn out on to a serving dish. Garnish with holly.

TIP
Let a pudding rest long enough for most of the steam to escape before unmould-ing it. Then it will be less likely to crack.

Oranges in Caramel Sauce

THE APPEAL OF THIS REFRESHING DESSERT is its lightness after a heavy Christmas feast. Made in advance, it is easy and convenient for entertaining.

Makes 6 servings

INGREDIENTS
6 large seedless oranges
115g/4oz/½ cup sugar
75ml/5 tbsp water

1   On a board, using a sharp knife, cut a slice from the top and the base of each orange. Cut off the peel in strips from the top to the base, following the contours of the fruit.

2   Slice the peeled oranges into rounds 1cm/ ½in thick. Arrange the sliced oranges in a serving bowl and add any juice.

3   With a sharp knife, remove the pith from a few pieces of the orange rind. Stack two or three pieces at a time and cut into julienne strips.

4   Half-fill a large bowl with cold water and set aside.

5   Place the sugar and 45ml/3 tbsp of water in a small, heavy saucepan without a non-stick coating and bring to the boil over a high heat, swirling the pan to dissolve the sugar. Boil, without stirring, until the mixture turns a dark caramel colour. Do not let it burn.

6   Remove from the heat and, standing back, dip the base of the pan into the cold water to stop the caramel from cooking.

7   Add 30ml/2 tbsp water, pouring it down the sides of the pan, and swirl to combine. Add the strips of orange rind and return the pan to the heat.

8   Simmer the orange rind over a medium-low heat, stirring occasionally, for 8–10 minutes, until slightly translucent.

9   Pour the caramel and rind over the oranges and turn gently to coat. Chill for at least 1 hour before serving.

Frozen Grand Marnier Soufflés

THESE SOPHISTICATED LITTLE DESSERTS are always appreciated and make a wonderful end to a meal.

Makes 8 servings

INGREDIENTS

225g/8oz/1 cup caster
    (superfine) sugar
6 large eggs, separated
250ml/8fl oz/1 cup milk
15g/½oz gelatine, soaked in
    45ml/3 tbsp water
475ml/16fl oz/2 cups double
    (heavy) cream
Grand Marnier

1 Tie double collars of greaseproof (waxed) paper around eight rame-kins. Whisk 75g/3oz/ 6 tbsp of sugar with the egg yolks until pale.

2 Heat the milk in a small saucepan until almost boiling and pour it on to the yolks, whisking constantly. Return to the pan.

3 Stir the mixture over a low heat until it coats the back of a spoon.

4 Remove the pan from the heat. Stir the soaked gelatine into the custard and stir until dissolved. Pour into a bowl and cool. Whisk occasionally until the custard is almost set.

5 Place the remaining sugar in a pan with 75ml/ 5 tbsp water and dissolve it over a low heat.

6 Bring to the boil, and boil until it reaches the soft-ball stage (119°C/240°F on a sugar thermometer). Remove from the heat. In a clean bowl, whisk the egg whites until stiff. Pour the hot syrup over the whites, whisking. Leave to cool.

7 Whisk the cream into soft peaks. Add 50ml/2fl oz/¼ cup Grand Marnier to the cooled custard and fold the custard into the egg whites, along with the whipped cream. Pour into the ramekins. Freeze overnight. Carefully remove the collars, then allow to sit at room temperature for 30 minutes before serving.

Moist and Rich Christmas Cake

The cake can be made 4 to 6 weeks before Christmas. During this time, pierce the cake with a fine needle and spoon a little brandy over it. Try to do this once a week until it is decorated.

Makes 1 cake

INGREDIENTS

225g/8oz/1⅓ cups sultanas
    (golden raisins)
225g/8oz/1 cup currants
225g/8oz/1⅓ cups raisins
115g/4oz/½ cup prunes,
    stoned (pitted) and chopped
50g/2oz/¼ cup glacé
    (candied) cherries
50g/2oz/⅓ cup chopped,
    mixed candied citrus peel
45ml/3 tbsp brandy or sherry
225g/8oz/2 cups plain flour
pinch of salt
2.5ml/½ tsp ground cinnamon
2.5ml/½ tsp grated nutmeg
15ml/1 tbsp cocoa powder
225g/8oz/1 cup butter
225g/8oz/1 cup dark
    brown sugar
4 large eggs
finely grated rind of 1 orange
115g/4oz/1⅓ cup ground
    almonds
50g/2oz/½ cup chopped
    almonds

TO DECORATE

60ml/4 tbsp apricot jam
450g/1lb almond paste
450g/1lb fondant icing
icing sugar, for dusting

1 The day before baking, place the fruit and spirit in a bowl. Cover and leave overnight. Grease a 20cm/8in round tin and line with a double thickness of greaseproof (waxed) paper.

2 Preheat the oven to 160°C/325°F/Gas 3. Sift together the flour, salt, spices and cocoa powder. In a separate bowl, cream the butter and sugar; beat in the eggs. Stir in the rind, almonds and dried fruit.

3 Fold in the flour mixture. Spoon into the tin.

4 Level the top and give the cake tin a gentle tap to knock out any air bubbles. Bake for 3 hours, or until a skewer inserted in to the centre comes out clean.

5 Cool the cake in the tin on a wire rack for 1 hour. Turn the cake out on to the rack, but leave the paper on, to keep it moist. When the cake is cool, wrap it in foil and store in a cool place.

6 Several days before serving, warm the apricot jam, then strain to make a glaze. Remove the paper from the cake and brush it with hot apricot glaze.

7 Cover the cake with a layer of almond paste, and leave to dry for 24 hours.

8 Cover with a layer of fondant icing. Tie a ribbon around the sides.

9 Roll out the fondant and stamp out 12 small holly leaves with a cutter.

10 Make one bell motif with a cookie cutter dusted with sifted icing sugar. Roll small balls for holly berries and allow them to dry on waxed paper for 24 hours. Decorate the cake with the leaves, berries and bell.

Novelty Christmas Cakes

THESE INDIVIDUAL CAKES can be packed in their own little boxes to make unusual gifts for children.

Makes 2 cakes

INGREDIENTS

115g/4oz/1 cup self-raising flour
5g/1 tsp baking powder
15g/½oz/1 tbsp cocoa powder
115g/4oz/½ cup caster (superfine) sugar
115g/4oz/½ cup soft margarine
2 eggs

TO DECORATE

45ml/3 tbsp apricot jam glaze
2 x 15cm/6in round cake boards
350g/12oz ready-made fondant icing
350g/12oz white marzipan
food colourings
glitter flakes (sugar crystals)

1 Preheat the oven to 160°C/325°F/ Gas 3. Grease and line two 15cm/6in round sandwich tins (cake pans). Place all the cake ingredients in a mixing bowl. Mix together with a wooden spoon and beat for 2–3 minutes.

3 Brush the apricot glaze over the cakes and place them on the cake boards. To make the clown, roll out one-third of the icing to a round large enough to cover one cake. Smooth the icing over the cake and trim at the base. Mould two ears and press into position. Colour one-third of the marzipan red and shape a mouth and nose; reserve the remainder. Colour a small piece of marzipan black and roll out thin lengths to outline the mouth and make the eyes and eyebrows.

2 Divide the mixture between the tins, smooth the tops and bake for 20–25 minutes or until ready. Allow the cakes to cool on a wire rack. Remove the paper.

4 Colour another small piece of marzipan yellow and grate coarsely for the hair. Colour another piece green for the ruffle. Stick in position with apricot glaze and sprinkle with white glitter flakes (sugar crystals).

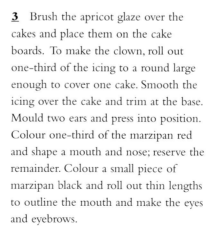

5 To make the Santa Claus cake, colour the remaining marzipan a skin tone, using brown colouring, and roll out thinly to cover two-thirds of the second cake. Trim. Roll out three-quarters of the red marzipan thinly and cover the remainder of the cake. Gather the excess at one side to make the hat. Mould a nose and mouth from the remaining red marzipan. Coarsely grate the remaining white icing and use to trim the hat and for the beard, moustache and eyebrows. Gently shape grated white icing into a small pom-pom for the hat. Shape two black eyes and press in position. Sprinkle red glitter flakes on to the hat.

TIP

To make the apricot jam glaze, add 30ml/2 tbsp water to 45ml/3 tbsp apricot jam in a small pan. Heat gently, stirring, to melt the jam, and sieve.

Edible Gifts

Delight your family and friends with
this luxurious connoisseur's collection
of irresistible seasonal treats.

FRUITS IN LIQUEURS

MAKE THESE BEAUTIFUL PRESERVES when the fruits are in season and store them away to make luxurious Christmas gifts.

Makes 450g/1lb

INGREDIENTS

450g/1lb fresh fruit such as apricots,
clementines, kumquats, cherries,
raspberries, peaches, plums or
seedless grapes
225g/8oz/1 cup granulated sugar
300ml/½ pint/1¼ cups water
150ml/¼ pint/⅔ cup liqueur
or spirit (alcohol such as rum, brandy,
Kirsch or Cointreau)

1 Wash the fruit. Halve and stone (pit) the apricots, plums and peaches. Prick the kumquats, cherries and grapes all over with a cocktail stick (toothpick). Pare the rind from the clementines and remove any white pith.

2 Place half the sugar in a saucepan with the water. Heat gently, stirring until the sugar has dissolved. Bring to the boil. Add the fruit to the syrup and simmer gently for 1–2 minutes until the fruit is just tender but still whole.

3 Carefully remove the fruit using a slotted spoon and arrange neatly in warmed, sterilized jars. Add the remaining sugar to the syrup in the pan and stir until it has dissolved completely.

4 Boil the syrup rapidly until it reaches the thread stage. Test by pressing a small amount of syrup between two spoons: when they pull apart a thread should form. Allow to cool.

5 Measure the cooled syrup, then add an equal quantity of liqueur or spirit (alcohol) and mix together. Pour over the fruit until covered. Seal each jar, label and keep for up to 4 months.

CHRISTMAS CHUTNEY

THIS CHUTNEY HAS A SWEET, BUT SPICY, FLAVOUR and makes the perfect accompaniment to cold meats, pâtés and cheese.

Makes 1.75kg/4–4½lb

INGREDIENTS
450g/1lb/9 plums, stoned (pitted)
450g/1lb/6 pears, peeled and cored
225g/8oz/2 cooking apples, peeled
* and cored*
225g/8oz/4 sticks celery
450g/1lb onions, sliced
450g/1lb tomatoes, skinned
115g/4oz/½ cup raisins
15g/½oz/1 tbsp grated fresh ginger
30ml/2 tbsp pickling spice
900ml/1½ pints/3¾ cups cider vinegar
450g/1lb/2¼ cups sugar

1   Chop the plums, pears, apples, celery and onions, and cut the tomatoes into quarters. Place all these ingredients, together with the raisins and ginger, in a very large saucepan.

2   Wrap the pickling spice in muslin and secure with string. Add to the saucepan with half the vinegar and bring to the boil. Cook for about 2 hours, giving the mixture an occasional stir.

3   Meanwhile, sterilize some jars and plastic lids. When all the ingredients are tender, stir in the remaining vinegar and the sugar. Boil until thick, remove the bag of spices and fill each jar with chutney. Cover with a wax paper disc and a lid. Label when cold.

CRAB APPLE AND LAVENDER JELLY

SUSPEND FRESH LAVENDER in the jar for an unusual presentation.

INGREDIENTS
900g/2lb crab apples
1.75 litres/3 pints/7½ cups water
lavender stems
900g/2lb/4½ cups sugar

1 Cut the fruit into chunks. Place in a preserving pan with the water and two lavender stems. Bring to the boil, cover the pan, and simmer for 1 hour. Stir occasionally, until the fruit is pulpy.

2 Pour the contents of the pan slowly into a suspended, sterilized jelly bag and leave to drip through slowly for several hours. Do not squeeze the bag or the jelly will become cloudy.

3 Discard the pulp and measure the juice in the bowl. To each 600ml/ 1 pint/2½ cups juice, add 450g/1lb/ 2¼ cups sugar and pour into a clean pan. Sterilize the jars and lids. This recipe makes sufficient to fill two 450g/1lb jars.

4 Heat the juice gently, stirring, until the sugar has dissolved. Bring to the boil and boil rapidly for 8–10 minutes until the setting point of 105°C/221°F is reached. Test this by putting a small amount of jelly on a cold plate. When cool, its surface should wrinkle when you push your finger through it.

5 Remove the pan from the heat and use a slotted spoon to remove froth from the surface. Carefully pour or ladle the jelly into a jug, then fill the warm, sterilized jars. Quickly dip some lavender stems into boiling water and insert one stem into each jar. Cover with discs of waxed paper and seal.

SALMON PATE

Delicate fresh salmon pâté wrapped in slices of smoked salmon makes a luxurious gift packed in a pretty dish. Store the pâté in the fridge to keep.

Makes 4

INGREDIENTS
350g/12oz fresh salmon fillet
15g/½oz/1 tbsp chopped fresh dill, plus
* sprigs to garnish*
115g/4oz/4 slices smoked salmon
115g/4oz/½ cup curd (cottage) or cream
* cheese*
75g/3oz/6 tbsp unsalted (sweet) butter
50g/2oz/1 cup fresh white breadcrumbs
5ml/1 tsp lemon juice
30ml/2 tbsp Madeira
salt and freshly ground black pepper

1 Preheat the oven to 190°C/375°F/ Gas 5. Put the salmon fillet on a sheet of greaseproof (waxed) paper on top of a sheet of foil. Sprinkle with salt, pepper and dill. Seal and bake for 10 minutes, until tender. Allow to cool and remove the skin. Save any juices.

2 Cut out four pieces of smoked salmon to fit the bases of four individual ramekin dishes. Cut out four more pieces the same size, to cover the pâté, and reserve. From the remaining smoked salmon, cut strips to fit around the inside edges of each dish. Cover the dishes and chill.

3 Place the cooked salmon and its juices in a food processor with the curd (cottage) or cream cheese, butter, breadcrumbs, lemon juice and Madeira. Process until smooth. Divide the mixture evenly between the ramekin dishes and level the surfaces. Cover with the reserved smoked salmon and decorate with sprigs of dill. Cover with clear film (plastic wrap) and chill.

Anchovy Spread

THIS DELICIOUS SPREAD has a concentrated flavour – perfect on toast.

Makes 600ml/1 pint/2½ cups

INGREDIENTS
2 x 50g/2oz cans anchovies in olive oil
4 garlic cloves, crushed
2 egg yolks
30ml/2 tbsp red wine vinegar
300ml/½ pint/1¼ cups olive oil
freshly ground black pepper
30g/1¼oz/½ cup fresh basil or thyme

1 Drain the oil from the anchovies and reserve. Place the anchovies and garlic in a food processor. Process until smooth. Add the egg yolks and vinegar, and process until the egg and vinegar have been absorbed by the anchovies.

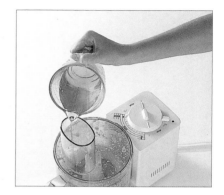

2 Pour the olive oil into a measuring jug (cup) and add the reserved anchovy oil. Set the food processor to a low speed and add the oil, drop by drop, to the anchovy mixture until it is thick and smooth.

3 Add some freshly ground black pepper and chopped fresh herbs, and blend until smooth. Spoon the mixture into small, sterilized jars, cover and label. Store in the fridge.

BELL PEPPERS IN OLIVE OIL

THE WONDERFUL FLAVOUR AND COLOUR of these bell peppers will add a Mediterranean theme to festive foods.

Makes enough to fill three
450g/1lb jars

INGREDIENTS
3 red bell peppers
3 yellow bell peppers
3 green bell peppers
300ml/½ pint/1¼ cups olive oil
pinch of salt
freshly ground black pepper
3 thyme sprigs

TIP
Choose interesting jars that can be used again and again, long after the delicious contents have gone.

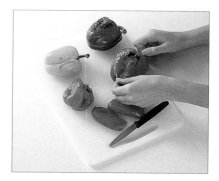

1   Prepare a hot grill (broiler) or pre-heat the oven to 200°C/400°F/Gas 6. Put the whole peppers on a grill rack (broiler pan) or baking sheet. Place under the heat for about 10 minutes until the skins are charred and blistered all over. Turn frequently during cooking.

2   Allow the peppers to cool for at least 5 minutes, then peel off the skins. Remove the cores, seeds and stalks. Slice each of the peppers thinly, keeping each colour separate, and place each in its own dish.

3   Pour one-third of the olive oil over each dish of peppers. Sprinkle with the salt and pepper and add a sprig of thyme to each dish. Stir to blend well. Sterilize three jars and lids and fill with peppers. Top up each jar with the oil. Seal and label.

CHOCOLATE TRUFFLES

SERVE THESE RICH, FRESH CREAM TRUFFLES with after-dinner coffee, or wrap lavishly to make a sumptuous gift.

Makes 20–30

INGREDIENTS

175ml/6fl oz/¾ cup double (heavy) cream
275g/10oz plain (semi-sweet) chocolate,
* chopped*
25g/1oz/2 tbsp unsalted (sweet) butter,
* cut into pieces*
30–45ml/2–3 tbsp brandy (optional)
cocoa powder
finely chopped pistachio nuts or hazelnuts

1 Bring the cream to the boil over a medium heat. Remove from the heat and add the chocolate, then stir until melted and smooth. Stir in the butter and the brandy, if using, then strain into a bowl and leave to cool. Cover and chill for 6–8 hours or overnight.

2 Line a large baking sheet with greaseproof (waxed) paper. Using a small ice-cream scoop or two teaspoons, form the chocolate mixture into 20–30 balls and place on the paper. Chill again if the mixture becomes too soft while you are moulding the truffles.

3 To coat the truffles with cocoa, sift the cocoa powder into a small bowl, drop in the truffles one at a time and roll to coat well, keeping the round shape. To coat with nuts, roll the truffles in finely chopped nuts.

VARIATION

To coat with chocolate, freeze the truffles for at least 1 hour. Melt 400g/14oz of dark, milk or white chocolate, then allow to cool slightly. Using a fork, dip each frozen truffle into the cooled chocolate. Place on baking parchment and chill.

GINGERBREAD HOUSE

THIS GINGERBREAD HOUSE makes a memorable party centrepiece, especially if it is filled with little gifts and surprises.

Makes 1 house

INGREDIENTS

90ml/6 tbsp golden (corn) syrup
30ml/2 tbsp black treacle (molasses)
75g/3oz/⅓ cup soft light brown sugar
75g/3oz/6 tbsp butter
450g/1lb/4 cups plain flour
15g/½oz/1 tbsp ground ginger
15g/½oz/1 tbsp bicarbonate of soda
   (baking soda)
2 egg yolks
barley sugar sweets (hard candies)

TO DECORATE

royal icing
25cm/10in square silver cake board
icing sugar, for dusting
1.5m/1½yds ribbon

PREPARATION

**Before you make the ginger-
bread, cut the following
shapes from stiff cardboard:
For the side walls: 2
rectangles 15 x 10cm/
6 x 4in. For the end walls:
2 rectangles 18 x 10cm/
7 x 4in, then mark a point
10cm/4in up each long side.
Mark the centre of the top
edge. Draw lines from here to
each of the side points, and
cut out. For the roof: 2 rectangles 20 x 15cm/8 x 6in.**

1   Preheat the oven to 190°C/375°F/
Gas 5. Line several baking sheets with
baking parchment. Heat the syrup,
treacle (molasses), sugar and butter in a
saucepan. Stir occasionally, until melted.

2   Sift the flour, ginger and
bicarbonate of soda (baking soda) into a
bowl. Add the yolks and pour in the
syrup mixture. Knead on a lightly
floured surface until smooth.

3   Roll out one-third of the dough
thinly. Reserve the rest in a plastic bag.
Cut out two end walls. Stamp out a
window using a 2.5cm/1in round cutter
and a door using a 2.5cm/1in square
cutter. Place a sweet (candy) in each
opening. Bake for 8–10 minutes. Cool.

4   Use the remaining dough to make
the two side walls and the two roof
pieces. Using the square cutter, stamp
out two windows in each wall. Using
the round cutter, stamp out three
windows in each roof piece. Decorate
and bake as before.

5 To decorate, pipe lines, loops and circles around the windows, doors and on the walls and roof with royal icing. Pipe beads of icing in groups of three all over the rest of the house. Leave to dry.

6 To assemble the house, pipe icing along the side edges of the walls and stick them together on the cake board. Pipe a line of icing following the pitch of the roof on both end pieces and along the top of the roof pieces. Press in position and support while the icing sets. Pipe the finishing touches to the roof and base. Dust the board with icing (confectioners') sugar to resemble snow. Wrap ribbon around the board.

Creamy Christmas Fudge

A BOX OF FUDGE IN A SELECTION OF FLAVOURS makes a good alternative to a box of chocolates.

Makes 900g (2lb)

INGREDIENTS
50g/2oz/4 tbsp unsalted (sweet) butter,
plus extra for greasing
450g/1lb/2¼ cups sugar
300ml/½ pint/1¼ cups double (heavy)
cream
150ml/¼ pint/⅔ cup milk
45ml/3 tbsp water (this can be replaced with
orange, apricot or cherry brandy,
or strong coffee)

FOR THE FLAVOURINGS
225g/8oz/1⅓ cup plain (semi-sweet)
or milk chocolate dots (chips)
115g/4oz/1 cup chopped almonds,
hazelnuts (filberts), walnuts or
Brazil nuts (optional)
115g/4oz/½ cup chopped glacé (candied)
cherries, dates or dried apricots (optional)
icing (confectioners') sugar, for dusting

1 Butter a 20cm/8in shallow square tin. Place the butter, sugar, cream, milk and water or other flavouring in a large, heavy-based saucepan. Heat very gently, stirring occasionally with a wooden spoon, until all the sugar has dissolved.

3 For chocolate-flavoured fudge, add the chocolate at this stage. Remove from the heat and beat. Alternatively, add chopped nuts or fruit and beat until the mixture thickens and is opaque.

2 Bring the mixture to the boil and boil steadily, stirring only occasionally to prevent it from burning on the base of the saucepan. Boil until the fudge reaches just under soft-ball stage (113°C/230°F for a soft fudge).

4 Pour the hot fudge into the prepared tin. Leave the mixture until cool and almost set. Using a sharp knife, mark the fudge into small squares. Leave in the tin until quite firm.

5 Turn the fudge out on to a board and invert. Using a long-bladed knife, cut into neat squares. You can dust some with icing (confectioners') sugar and drizzle others with melted chocolate if you wish.

> **TIP**
>
> A beautiful festive tin or gift box is the perfect finishing touch for this delicious gift.

Chocolate Christmas Cups

THESE TREATS ARE A PERFECT WAY of using up leftover Christmas pudding. To crystallize cranberries, beat an egg white until frothy; dip each berry in the egg white, then in caster (superfine) sugar. Dry on sheets of baking parchment.

Makes 30–35 cups

INGREDIENTS
275g/10oz plain (semi-sweet) chocolate,
  broken into pieces
70–80 foil or paper sweet (candy) cases
175g/6oz cooked, cold Christmas pudding
75ml/3fl oz/⅓ cup brandy or whisky
chocolate holly leaves and crystallized
  cranberries to decorate

1 Place the chocolate in a bowl over a pan of barely simmering water until it melts, stirring until smooth. Using a pastry brush, coat melted chocolate on to the inside of about 35 sweet (candy) cases. Allow to set, then apply a second coat, reheating the chocolate if necessary. Leave for 4–5 hours to set. Reserve the remaining chocolate.

2 Crumble the Christmas pudding into a small bowl. Sprinkle with brandy or whisky and allow to stand for 30–40 minutes, until the spirit (liquor) has been absorbed by the pudding crumbs.

3 Spoon pudding mixture into each cup, smoothing the top. Reheat the remaining chocolate and spoon over the top of each cup to cover the surface right to the edge. Leave to set.

4 When the chocolate cups are set, carefully peel off the sweet (candy) cases and replace them with clean ones. Decorate with chocolate holly leaves and crystallized cranberries.

Festive Florentines

Try these chewy ginger treats served with ice cream.

Makes 30

Ingredients

50g/2oz/4 tbsp butter
115g/4oz/8 tbsp caster (superfine) sugar
50g/2oz/¼ cup mixed glacé (candied) cherries, chopped
25g/1oz/2 rounded tbsp candied orange peel, chopped
50g/2oz/½ cup flaked (sliced) almonds
50g/2oz/½ cup chopped walnuts
25g/1oz/1 tbsp glacé (candied) ginger, chopped
30ml/2 tbsp (all-purpose) plain flour
2.5ml/½ tsp ground ginger

To Finish

50g/2oz dark chocolate
50g/2oz white chocolate

TIP

To keep these florentines in good condition, store them in an airtight container.

1 Preheat the oven to 180°C/350°F/ Gas 4. Whisk the butter and sugar together until they are light and fluffy. Thoroughly mix in all the remaining ingredients, except the chocolate.

3 Remove the biscuits (cookies) from the oven and flatten them with a wet fork, shaping them into neat rounds. Return to the oven for 3–4 minutes, until golden brown. Allow to cool on the baking sheets for 2 minutes, then transfer them to a wire rack.

2 Cut baking parchment to fit your baking sheets. Put four small spoonfuls of the mixture on each sheet, spacing them to allow for spreading. Flatten the mixture and bake for 5 minutes.

4 Break the dark chocolate into a bowl set over a pan of simmering water to melt. Stir until smooth. Spread the melted chocolate on one side of half the biscuits. Melt the white chocolate and spread on the undersides of the remaining biscuits.

CHRISTMAS COOKIES

USE EGG GLAZE TO PAINT bright, glossy motifs on these cookies.

Makes about 12

INGREDIENTS

75g/3oz/6 tbsp butter
50g/2oz/generous ½ cup icing (confectioners') sugar
finely grated rind of 1 small lemon
1 egg yolk
175g/6oz/1½ cups plain (all-purpose) flour
pinch of salt

TO DECORATE

2 egg yolks
food colouring in red and green

TIP

For an alternative flavouring, omit the lemon rind and add 25g/1oz/¼ cup ground almonds and a few drops of almond essence (extract). Pack the cookies into an airtight tin to make a lovely, festive gift.

1 In a large bowl, beat the butter, sugar and lemon rind together until pale and fluffy. Beat in the egg yolk, and sift in the flour and the salt. Knead to form a smooth dough. Wrap in plastic wrap and chill for 30 minutes.

3 Transfer the cookies to lightly greased baking trays. Mark the top of each one lightly with a 2.5cm/1in holly-leaf cutter. Use a 5mm/¼in plain piping nozzle to imprint the holly berries. Chill the cookies for at least 10 minutes, until firm.

2 Preheat the oven to 190°C/375°F/ Gas 5. On a lightly floured surface, roll out the dough to 3mm/⅛in thick. Using a 6cm/2½in fluted cutter, stamp out the cookies. Dip the cutter in flour to stop it from sticking to the dough.

4 Put each egg yolk into a cup. Mix red food colouring into one and green into the other. Paint the leaves and berries. Bake for 10–12 minutes, until the edges begin to colour. Let them cool slightly on the trays before transferring them to a wire rack.

Chocolate Nut Clusters

These delicious sweetmeats (candies) are very simple to make.

Makes about 30

Ingredients

525ml/17fl oz/2¼ cups double (heavy)
   cream
25g/1oz/2 tbsp unsalted (sweet) butter
350ml/12fl oz/1½ cups golden (corn) syrup
200g/7oz/1 cup sugar
90g/3½oz/½ cup soft light brown sugar
pinch of salt
15ml/1 tbsp vanilla essence (extract)
425g/15oz/3 cups hazelnuts, pecans,
   walnuts, Brazil nuts, unsalted peanuts
400g/14oz plain (semi-sweet) chocolate
25g/1oz/2 tbsp white vegetable fat (crisco)

Tip

Test for the "soft-ball stage" by spooning a small amount of caramel into a bowl of cold water: it should form a soft ball when rolled between finger and thumb.

1 Lightly oil two baking sheets. Cook the cream, butter, syrup, sugars and salt in a large, heavy-based saucepan over a medium heat until smooth, stirring occasionally. Bring to the boil and stir frequently until the caramel reaches 119°C/240°F (soft-ball stage).

3 Chill the clusters for 30 minutes. Melt the chocolate and vegetable fat (crisco) together in a pan over low heat. Stir until smooth. Cool slightly. Using a metal knife (spatula), transfer each to a wire rack set over a baking sheet.

2 Plunge the bottom of the pan into a bowl of cold water to stop cooking. Cool slightly, then stir in the vanilla essence (extract). Stir in the nuts until well coated. Using an oiled tablespoon, drop spoonfuls of the mixture on to the prepared sheets, about 2.5cm/1in apart.

4 Spoon chocolate over each cluster, covering it completely. Alternatively, use a fork to dip each cluster in the chocolate before returning it to the wire rack. Allow to set for 2 hours until hard. Store in an airtight container.

Chocolate Kisses

Dusted with sugar, these rich cookies look attractive on a plate. Serve with coffee, or ice cream.

Makes 24

Ingredients

*75g/3oz plain (semi-sweet) chocolate,
  broken into pieces*
75g/3oz white chocolate, broken into pieces
115g/4oz/½ cup butter
115g/4oz/8 tbsp caster (superfine) sugar
2 eggs
225g/8oz/2 cups plain flour
icing (confectioners') sugar, to decorate

1 Put each type of chocolate into a separate bowl and melt over a pan of barely simmering water. Leave to cool.

2 Whisk the butter and sugar until pale and fluffy. Beat in the eggs, one at a time. Sift in the flour and mix well.

3 Divide the mixture between the two bowls of chocolate. Thoroughly mix each chocolate in to the mixture. Knead the doughs until smooth, wrap them in clear film (plastic wrap) and chill for 1 hour. Preheat the oven to 190°C/375°F/Gas 5.

4 Take up slightly rounded teaspoonfuls of each dough and roll into balls in the palms of your hands. Arrange them on greased baking trays and bake for 10–12 minutes. Dust with sifted icing (confectioners') sugar and transfer to a wire rack to cool.

New Year Shortbread

This deliciously light Hogmanay, or New Year's Eve, shortbread is based on a traditional Scottish recipe.

Makes 2 large or 8 individual shortbreads

INGREDIENTS
175g/6oz/1⅔ cups plain flour
50g/2oz/¼ cup cornflour (cornstarch)
50g/2oz/¼ cup caster (superfine) sugar
115g/4oz/½ cup unsalted (sweet) butter
sugar, to decorate

1 Preheat the oven to 160°C/325°F/ Gas 3. Lightly flour a mould and line a baking sheet with baking parchment. Sift the flour, cornflour (cornstarch) and sugar into a mixing bowl. Cut the butter into pieces and rub into the flour mixture until dough-like.

2 Place some dough in the mould and press to fit. Invert the mould on to the baking sheet and tap firmly to release the dough shape. Repeat with the rest of the dough. Bake for 35–40 minutes or until the shortbread is pale golden in colour.

3 Sprinkle the top of the shortbread with a little sugar and cool on the baking sheet. Wrap in cellophane or pack in a box tied with ribbon.

TIP
Handle the dough as little as possible to avoid making the shortbread tough. If you do not have a wooden mould, press the dough into a round flan tin (tart pan) or ring and crimp the edges.

INDIVIDUAL DUNDEE CAKES

DUNDEE CAKES ARE TRADITIONALLY TOPPED with almonds, but look tempting covered with candied fruits. One of these small cakes would make a charming gift for someone living alone, or could be included in a Christmas hamper (package).

Makes 3 cakes

INGREDIENTS

225g/8oz/1½ cup raisins
225g/8oz/1 cup currants
225g/8oz/1½ cup sultanas (golden raisins)
50g/2oz/¼ cup glacé (candied) cherries,
*   sliced*
115g/4oz/¾ cup candied mixed fruit peel
grated rind of 1 orange
300g/11oz/2⅔ cups plain flour
2.5ml/½ tsp baking powder
5ml/1 tsp ground mixed spice (allspice)
225g/8oz/1 cup unsalted (sweet) butter
225g/8oz/1 cup caster (superfine) sugar
5 eggs

FOR THE TOPPING

50g/2oz/⅓ cup whole blanched almonds
50g/2oz/¼ cup glacé (candied) cherries,
*   halved*
50g/2oz/½ cup glacé (candied) fruits, sliced
45ml/3 tbsp apricot jam

TIP

To make a glaze for the tops of the cakes, add 30ml/ 2 tbsp water to the apricot jam in a small pan. Heat gently, stirring, to melt the jam, and sieve.

1 Preheat the oven to 150°C/300°F/ Gas 2. Grease and line three 15cm/6in round cake tins and tie a strip of brown paper around each. Mix all the fruit and the orange rind in a large mixing bowl. In another bowl, sift the flour, baking powder and mixed spice (allspice). Add the butter, sugar and eggs. Mix with a wooden spoon and beat for 2–3 minutes until smooth and glossy.

2 Add the mixed fruit to the cake mixture and fold in. Divide the mixture between the three tins. Level the tops. Arrange the almonds in circles over the top of one cake, the glacé (candied) cherries over the second cake and the mixed glacé (candied) fruit peel over the last one. Bake for 2–2½ hours or until a skewer inserted into the centre of the cakes comes out clean.

3 Leave the cakes in their tins until completely cold. Turn out, remove the lining paper and brush the tops with apricot glaze. Leave to set, then wrap in cellophane or clear film (plastic wrap) and pack in pretty boxes or tins.

CANDIED FRUIT

MAKE CANDIED PEEL WHEN THE NEW SEASON'S CITRUS FRUIT IS AVAILABLE. Any syrup that is left over from the candying process can be used in fruit salads or drizzled over a freshly baked sponge cake. To preserve the flavour of each fruit, candy each type separately. It will keep well in an airtight jar.

CANDIED CITRUS PEEL

Makes about 675g/1½lb

INGREDIENTS
5 large oranges or 10 lemons
or limes, unwaxed
675g/1½lb/3½ cups sugar,
plus extra for sprinkling

1 Halve the fruit, squeeze out the juice and discard the flesh, but not the pith. Cut the peel into thin strips.

2 Place in a pan, cover with boiling water and simmer for 5 minutes.

3 Drain, then repeat step 2 four times, using fresh water each time.

4 In a heavy saucepan, combine 250ml/8fl oz/ 1 cup water and the sugar; heat to dissolve the sugar. Add the peel and cook slowly, partially covered, until soft (30–40 minutes). Cool thoroughly; sprinkle with sugar.

CANDIED GINGER

Makes about 675g/1½lb

INGREDIENTS
350g/12oz fresh ginger
225g/8oz/1 cup sugar
caster (superfine) sugar, for
coating

1 Place the ginger in a pan. Cover with water, bring to the boil and simmer for 15 minutes.

2 Drain the ginger. Peel when cool. Cut into 5mm/¼in slices.

3 In a heavy saucepan, dissolve the sugar in 120ml/4fl oz/½ cup water and cook, without stirring, over a low heat until the mixture becomes syrupy – about 15 minutes. Add the ginger and continue to cook gently until the ginger has absorbed the syrup. Shake the pan occasionally to prevent it from sticking. Remove the cooked slices and place them on a wire rack.

4 When cool, coat the ginger slices with caster (superfine) sugar. Spread them on greaseproof (waxed) paper for 2–3 days, until crystallized.

FESTIVE LIQUEURS

THESE ARE EASIER TO MAKE THAN WINES AND MAY BE made with a variety of flavourings and spirits (alcohols). All these liqueurs should mature for three months before drinking. Each recipe makes 1 litre/1¾ pints/4 cups.

PLUM BRANDY

450g/1lb plums, pitted
225g/8oz/1 cup brown sugar
600ml/1 pint/2½ cups
* brandy*

1   Slice the plums. Place in a sterilized jar with the sugar and brandy. Crack three stones (pits), remove the kernels and chop. Add to the jar.

2   Cover and store in a cool place for 3 months, shaking daily for 2 weeks and occasionally after that.

FRUIT GIN

450g/1lb/2⅔ cups raspberries
* or blackcurrants*
350g/12oz/1¾ cups sugar
750ml/1¼ pints/3 cups gin

Place the fruit in a sterilized jar. Add the sugar and gin and stir until well blended. Cover and store as for Plum Brandy.

BOTTLING LIQUEURS

Sterilize the bottles and corks or stoppers for each liqueur.

When the liqueurs are ready to be bottled, strain, then pour into the bottles through a funnel fitted with a filter paper. Fit with the corks or stoppers and attach decorative labels to the bottles.

CITRUS WHISKY

1 large orange
1 small lemon
1 lime
225g/8oz/1 cup sugar
600ml/1 pint/2½ cups
* whisky*

1   Using a sharp knife or a vegetable peeler, pare the rind from the fruit. Squeeze out all the juice, and place in a sterilized jar with the rinds.

2   Add the sugar and whisky and stir until well blended. Cover and store as for Plum Brandy.

FLORAL DECORATIONS

Savour the fragrance and beauty of natural decorations: luxuriant evergreens, gilded fruit and fresh flowers.

Nut and Cone Garland

THIS WINTRY GARLAND is very simple and quick to make.

YOU WILL NEED

glue gun and fir (pine) cones
ready-made vine garland
Brazil nuts, walnuts and
    hazelnuts (filberts)
red paper ribbon
stub (floral) wire

TIP

When the garland of nuts and cones is beginning to look a little tired, you can freshen it up with a coat of spray paint. Silver, gold and white provide the most successful frosting effect because some of the natural colour of the materials in the garland will show through from underneath the paint.

1 Using a glue gun, simply stick the various items to the vine garland, beginning with the fir (or pine) cones. Glue them to the ring in groups of 4–5, leaving a good space between each group. Stick larger cones to the bottom of the garland and use any smaller ones on the sides and the top.

2 Add the nuts either in groups of one variety only or mixed together. Make sure that you fill the spaces between the cones to hide the ring. Arrange the items so that they graduate from a thin layer at the top of the ring to a thicker one at the bottom.

3 Once all the items have been added to the garland, add the finishing touches. To secure the paper ribbon in place, either pass a stub (floral) wire through the back of the knot and thread the wire through the ring, or simply glue the bow in place. For a different effect, you can spray the bow lightly with gold paint.

Blue Pine Christmas Candle

You Will Need

knife

florist's dry foam block

terracotta flowerpot

candle

hay

secateurs (pruning shears)

blue pine (spruce)

stub (floral) wires

reindeer moss

mossing (floral) pins

dried roses, pine cones, kutchi fruit, and dried mushrooms

Tip

Never leave a display with a lighted candle burning unattended. When creating a design, always ensure that the dried materials are as far away from the candle as possible.

1 Trim the foam block so that it fits tightly in the pot and insert the candle. Pack any space around the foam with hay. Trim the needles from the base of each blue pine (spruce) stem, to make it easier to insert into the foam. Starting at the base, position the largest pieces so that they lean down slightly.

3 Fill any large spaces in the display with moss, holding it in place with mossing (floral) pins. Put plenty of moss around the base of the candle, to cover any fixings (wires).

2 Add more larger pieces all around the pot. Using shorter lengths, add a layer above the first. Continue until the final and shortest layer is added, nearest to the candle. When adding the smaller pieces, use a stub (floral) wire to give strength or length. Keep the foliage away from the base of the candle.

4 Wire the roses into bunches of two or three. Wire the pine cones, kutchi fruit and dried mushrooms. Add the wired materials, using them to fill any spaces in the foliage.

Mistletoe Kissing Ring

INSTEAD OF JUST TYING A BUNCH OF MISTLETOE to some strategically placed light fitting in the hall, be creative and make a traditional kissing ring. This can be hung up as a Christmas decoration and still serve as a focal point for a seasonal kiss!

YOU WILL NEED

scissors and twine
7 berries-only stems of
    winterberry
large bunch mistletoe
1 twisted wicker wreath
roll of tartan (plaid) ribbon

TIP

Very simple in its construction, this design requires a reasonable quantity of good quality, fresh mistletoe to survive the full festive season.

1 Cut the stems of the winterberry into 18cm/7in lengths. Divide the mistletoe into 14 substantial stems and make the smaller sprigs into bunches by tying with twine. Attach a branch of winterberry to the outside of the wreath with the twine. Add a stem or bunch of mistletoe so that it overlaps about one-third of the winterberry, and bind in place. Bind on another stem of winterberry, overlapping the mistletoe.

2 Repeat the sequence until the outside of the cane ring is covered in a herringbone pattern of materials. Cut four lengths of ribbon of approximately 60cm/24in each. Tie one end of each of the pieces of ribbon to the decorated ring at four equidistant points. Bring the four ends of the ribbon up above the ring and tie into a bow; this will enable you to suspend the finished kissing ring in position.

Classic Clove and Orange Pomanders

THE TRADITIONAL POMANDER starts as a fresh orange and dries into a beautiful decoration with a warm, spicy smell evocative of mulled wine. Hang them around the home, or put in a wardrobe (closet) to scent its contents.

YOU WILL NEED

3 contrasting lengths of ribbon
3 small, firm oranges
cloves
scissors

1 Tie a length of ribbon around each orange as if you were tying it around a parcel. Cross it over at the base and bring the ends up to the top of the orange.

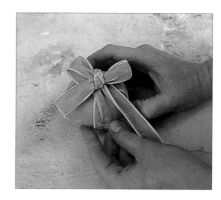

2 Finish off by tying the ribbon into a bow. Adjust the position of the ribbon as necessary to ensure that the orange is divided into four equal-sized sections.

3 Starting at the edges of the sections, push the sharp ends of the cloves into the exposed orange skin and continue until each quarter is completely covered. Trim the ends of the ribbon.

TIP

The oranges will shrink as they dry out so you will probably need to tighten the ribbons and re-tie the bows.

Herbal Potpourri

You Will Need

1 handful dried mint leaves

2 handfuls dried marigold flowers

1 handful of either thyme, sage or marjoram

10 dried orange slices

6 cinnamon sticks

a few dried chillies

4 nutmegs

5ml/1 tsp mint essential oil

15ml/1 tbsp sweet orange essential oil

mixing bowl and spoon

large plastic bag

15ml/1 tbsp ground orris root

1 Combine all the ingredients, except the orris root, in the bowl. Make sure the oils are well mixed in.

2 Transfer the mixture to a large plastic bag, add the orris root and shake well. Tie to close. Leave to mature for 1–2 weeks, shaking occasionally. Then transfer the mixture into a suitable bowl or dish to display it.

Rose-scented Bags

A TRANSLUCENT, GOSSAMER FABRIC MADE into a simple bag and filled with scented rose petals will scent a room deliciously as well as looking decorative. Add a few drops of rose essential oil from time to time.

1 Pin the two fabric pieces right sides together. Sew around all four sides, leaving a 3cm/1¼in gap on one side. Turn the bag through the gap so that it is right side out.

2 Press all four seams and slip-stitch the small gap closed. About one-quarter of the way down, run two lines of stitches across the width of the bag, about 2cm/⅜in apart, to accommodate the drawstring.

You Will Need

FOR A BAG ABOUT
15 x 20CM/6 x 8IN

outer fabric, 35 x 23cm/14 x 9in

lining fabric, 35 x 23cm/14 x 9in

pins

needle and thread

scissors

adhesive tape

length of cord, 40cm/16in

2 matching tassels

dried, scented rose petals

3 Fold the bag in half with the right sides together. Sew up the bag bottom and side (by hand or with a sewing machine). Turn right sides out and press flat.

4 At the side seam, make a small snip in the outer fabric to pull the drawstring through. Wind a piece of adhesive tape around the end of the cord to prevent it from fraying and feed it into the gap in the seam. Feed it all the way around the bag and out at the other side through another small hole in the casing. Tie a single loop in each end of the cord and attach a matching tassel.

5 Fill the bag with scented rose petals. Pull the cord to create gathers in the neck of the bag. Tie a knot to secure the bag and neaten any edges.

HEART-SHAPED WREATH

JUST BEND TWIGS INTO A HEART SHAPE and adorn it with ivy, berries and a white rose for a stunning door wreath.

YOU WILL NEED

secateurs (pruning shears)
pliable branches
florist's silver reel wire
seagrass rope
variegated ivy trails (sprigs)
red berries
tree ivy
picture framer's wax gilt
white rose or Christmas rose
golden twine

1 Using secateurs (pruning shears), cut six lengths of pliable branches, each about 70cm/28in long. Wire three branches together at one end. Repeat with the other three. Cross the two bundles over at the wired end, then wire the bunches together in the crossed-over position.

2 Holding the crossed, wired ends with one hand, ease the long end around and down very gently, so the branches don't snap. Repeat with the other side, to form a heart shape. Wire the bottom end of the heart.

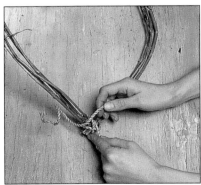

3 Bind the wiring with seagrass rope at top and bottom, and make a hanging loop at the top.

4 Entwine trailing ivy around the heart. Add berries. Make a posy of tree ivy leaves (gild them using picture framer's wax gilt) and a rose. Tie the posy with golden twine. Wire the posy in position at the top of the heart.

Winter Table Swag

THIS FESTIVE SWAG of fresh blue pine (spruce) will dry out after a few days, but will retain its colour and all its needles.

YOU WILL NEED

scissors
rope
secateurs (pruning shears)
blue pine (spruce)
florist's silver reel wire
cones
chillies
stub (floral) wires
glue gun
mushrooms
pomegranates
reindeer moss
lavender and red roses

1 Cut two lengths of rope; their combined length should be the length of the finished swag. Cut the blue pine (spruce) to about 20cm/8in long. Bind the stems to the rope with florist's wire.

2 If some cones are attached to the stems, bind them to the rope with florist's silver reel wire and continue to add the pine.

3 Continue until the whole length of both ropes has been covered. Don't leave gaps along the edges as you add the pine. Centre-wire the chillies with stub (floral) wire. Secure them along the length of the swag.

4 Glue the mushrooms, loose cones and pomegranates in place. Then add the reindeer moss.

5 Centre-wire the lavender and roses. Attach them in groups, crossing a bunch of roses with a bunch of lavender. Twist the loose wires under the swag and tuck the sharp ends back into the bottom of the swag.

GILDED FIG PYRAMID

AN ALMOST PROFLIGATE USE OF FIGS produces a gloriously decadent decoration for the festive table.

YOU WILL NEED

florist's dry foam cone
    approximately 25cm/
    10in high
gilded terracotta flowerpot
all-purpose glue
picture framer's wax gilt
40 black figs
stub (floral) wires
50 ivy leaves

1 Make sure that the dry foam cone sits comfortably in the pot. To ensure that it is stable, put a dab of glue around the edge of the cone base. Gild the figs slightly on one side of the fruit only, by rubbing the wax gilt on to the skin with your fingers.

2 Wire the gilded figs by pushing a stub (floral) wire horizontally through the flesh approximately 2.5cm/1in above the base of the fruit. Carefully bend the two protruding pieces of wire so that they point downwards. Take care not to tear the skin of the figs.

3 Attach the figs to the cone by pushing their wires into the dry foam. Work in concentric circles around the cone upwards from the bottom.

4 When you reach the top, position the last fig with its stem going upwards to create a point.

5 Make hairpin shapes out of the stub (floral) wires and insert the ivy leaves into the cone between the figs, covering any exposed foam.

CHRISTMAS CANDLE TABLE DECORATION

BRIGHT ANEMONES, RANUNCULUS AND HOLLY are set off by the grey of lichen on larch (pine) twigs and the soft green of aromatic rosemary. The simple white candles are given a festive lift with their individual bows.

YOU WILL NEED

25cm/10in florist's foam ring

25cm/10in wire basket with candleholders and candles

knife

10 stems rosemary

10 small stems lichen-covered larch (pine)

10 small stems holly

scissors

30 stems red anemones

30 stems red ranunculus

pleated paper ribbon

TIP

Never leave burning candles unattended and do not allow the candles to burn less than 5cm/2in above the display.

1 Soak the florist's foam ring in water and wedge it into the wire basket. If you need to trim the ring slightly, make sure that you do not cut too much off – it should fit snugly.

2 Use rosemary, larch (pine) and holly to create an even and textured twig outline, all around the foam ring. Make sure that the stems towards the outer ring are shorter than those in the centre.

3 Cut the stems of the anemones and ranunculus to 7.5cm/3in. Arrange them evenly throughout the display, leaving a little space around the candleholders. Make four ribbon bows and attach them to the candles. Position the candles in the holders.

Clementine Wreath

This vivid wreath will look spectacular hung on a door or wall. Set on its base, it can also be used as a table decoration with a large candle in the centre, or perhaps a cluster of smaller candles of staggered heights. The wreath is very easy to make, but it is heavy. If it is to be hung, be sure to attach it securely.

1 Push a stub (floral) wire through the base of a clementine from one side to the other, and bend the two projecting ends down. Bend another stub wire to form a hairpin shape and push the ends through the middle of the clementine so that the bend in the wire is sitting flush with the top of the fruit. Do the same with all the clementines. Trim all the projecting wires to a length of approximately 4cm/1½in.

2 Soak the florist's foam ring in water. Arrange the wired clementines in a tight circle on top of the plastic ring by pushing their four projecting wire legs into the foam. Form a second ring of clementines within the first ring.

3 Cut the pyracantha into small berry and foliage clusters approximately 6cm/2½in long. Push the stems into the outer side of the foam ring and between the two rings of clementines, making sure they are evenly distributed.

4 Cut the ivy leaves into individual stems measuring approximately 6cm/2½in long. Push the stems of the leaves into the ring, positioning a leaf between each clementine.

You Will Need
stub (floral) wires
30 clementines
wire cutters
30cm/12in florist's
    foam ring
pyracantha berries
    and foliage
scissors
ivy leaves

Small Fresh Rose Ring

WHILE THIS DELIGHTFUL FLORAL CIRCLET could be used at any time of the year, the impact created by the massed red roses makes it particularly romantic. With a candle at its centre, use it as a table decoration for a celebratory dinner.

YOU WILL NEED

15cm/6in diameter florist's foam ring
dark green ivy leaves
stub (floral) wires
bun moss
scissors
20 stems dark red roses

1 Soak the florist's foam ring in water. Push individual, medium-size ivy leaves into the foam to create an even foliage outline all around the ring.

2 Make U-shaped staples out of the stub (floral) wires and pin small pieces of bun moss on to the foam ring between the ivy leaves.

3 Cut the rose stems to about 4cm/1½in long and push them into the foam until the ring is evenly covered. The ivy should still be visible in between the rose heads.

TIP

If you receive a bouquet of red roses, why not recycle them? After the rose blooms have fully blown open, cut down their stems for use in this circlet to extend their lives. Finally, dehydrate the circlet and continue to use it as a dried flower display.

Everlasting Christmas Tree

THIS DELIGHTFUL LITTLE TREE is made from dyed, preserved oak leaves and decorated with tiny gilded cones.

YOU WILL NEED

knife
1 bunch of dyed, dried oak
    leaves
florist's silver reel wire
stub (floral) wires
small fir cones
picture framer's wax gilt
terracotta pot, 18cm/7in tall
small foam cone
florist's dry foam cone
    18cm/7in tall

TIP

You could make several small arrangements and then group them together to make a wonderfully festive centrepiece, or place one at each place setting.

1 Cut the leaves off the branches and trim the stalks. Wire up bunches of about four leaves, making some bunches with small leaves, some with medium-size leaves and others with large leaves. Sort the bunches into piles.

2 Insert a stub (floral) wire into the bottom end of each fir cone and twist the ends together. Gild each cone by rubbing on picture framer's wax gilt.

3 Prepare the pot by cutting the smaller foam cone to fit the pot, adding stub (floral) wire stakes and positioning the larger cone on to this. Attach the leaf bunches to the cone, starting at the top with the small leaves, and working down through the medium and large leaves to make a realistic shape. Add the gilded cones to finish.

Seasonal Decorations

Transform your surroundings — from tabletop to treetop and virtually every surface in between — into a Christmas wonderland.

White Christmas Tree

THIS ABSTRACT INTERPRETATION of the traditional tree looks best as part of a restrained white-and-gold arrangement.

YOU WILL NEED

glue gun and sisal string
**polystyrene (styrofoam) cone
    and star**
scissors and paintbrushes
white emulsion (latex) paint
gold paint

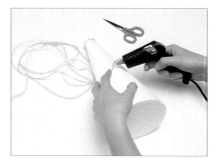

1 Glue the end of the string to the base of the cone. Wind the string up towards the point, then down to the base again, gluing it as you work. Each time you reach the base, cut the string and start again from another point.

2 When you have covered the cone evenly with string, wind a short length into a coil and glue it to the top of the cone to make a stable base for the star to sit on.

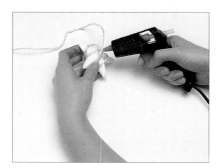

3 Wind and glue string around the star in the same way. Hide the raw ends under the star. Glue the star to the top of the cone.

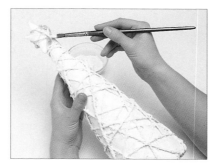

4 Paint the cone and star with several coats of white emulsion (latex) paint, covering the string and filling in any dips in the polystyrene (styrofoam).

5 Finish by brushing roughly over the string with gold paint.

"Baroque" Christmas Wreath

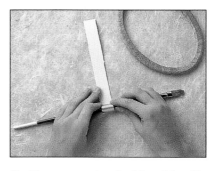

YOU WILL NEED

scissors and glue
gold crêpe paper
oval embroidery hoop
gold card (stock) and pencil
black felt-tip pen

1 Cut a long strip of gold crêpe paper and glue one end to the hoop. Wind the paper around the hoop to cover it.

2 Now cut a strip of gold card (stock) 1 x 30cm/½ x 12in and wrap it tightly around a pencil.

4 Using the template, scaled to the size required, draw the angel playing the trumpet on to the back of some gold card and cut out. Draw on the features with a black felt-tip pen. Make a bow out of gold crêpe paper and stick it on to the top of the wreath.

5 Glue the angel to the left-hand side of the wreath.

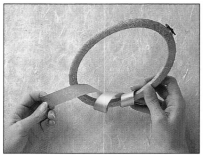

3 Attach one end of the curled gold strip halfway up the right-hand side of the hoop, wind around the hoop and attach the other end just beyond the bottom point.

Sparkling Table Toppers

At Christmas, dress your wineglasses for dinner. Lace fine gold wire around them, and add jewel-laden golden stripes and strings of gold beads to create simple, yet striking, table decorations. Add a tablecloth festooned with glittery, gold stars for a lavish, yet understated, effect.

JEWELLED GLASSES

1 "Lace" fine beading wire around the stem and bowl of a pretty wineglass or champagne flute. Taking care not to break the delicate wire by over-handling it, tie it around the stem to secure it to the glass. Once you are satisfied with the position, add a spot of glue.

2 Stick a length of masking tape long enough to go around the glass on to a piece of card (stock) and spray it with gold paint. Use a craft knife and metal ruler to cut it into thin strips. Attach a strip to each glass near the rim, and trim with a stick-on jewel. Wash these delicate glasses by hand. If you lose some of the decorations, apply new ones.

YOU WILL NEED
fine beading wire
stemmed glasses
all-purpose glue
masking tape
card
gold spray paint
cutting mat and
   craft knife
metal ruler
stick-on jewels
white voile to cover
   a table
artist's brush
gold paint

STARRY TABLECLOTH

1 Place a circular object on a piece of card and trace around it. Draw three lines for the star to make six equal sections.

2 Place the drawing under the voile and use an artist's brush to trace the star on to the cloth with gold paint. Repeat randomly over the entire tablecloth. Dry thoroughly.

Cinnamon Advent Candle

ADVENT CANDLES often have calibrations along their length to tell you how much to burn each day during the countdown to Christmas. This unusual advent candle has a novel way of marking the passage of time: a spiral of 25 cinnamon sticks, each of decreasing height. Every day, the candle is burnt down to the next cinnamon stick, until finally, on Christmas Day, it is level with the shortest. For a heady bonus, the heat of the burning flame releases the spicy aroma of the cinnamon. Dried red roses complete the festive look of the candle. Remember, never leave an advent candle – or any candle – burning unattended.

1 Attach the cinnamon sticks to the outside of the candle by strapping them on with raffia as shown.

2 Position the cinnamon sticks in equal height reductions so that they spiral around the candle from the highest at the top to the shortest at the bottom. (The shortest should come about 6cm/2½in up the candle.)

3 Using scissors, cut the excess lengths of cinnamon from the sticks so that they are all flush with the base of the candle.

4 Once the base is level, push the cinnamon-wrapped candle into the centre of the foam ring. Make hairpin shapes from the stub (floral) wires and pin the reindeer moss to the foam to cover the ring.

5 Cut the stems of the dried roses to a length of approximately 2.5cm/1in. Add a little glue to the bases and stems of the roses. Push them into the plastic foam through the reindeer moss to create a ring of roses around the candle.

YOU WILL NEED
25 medium-
    thickness
    cinnamon sticks
candle, 7.5 x 23cm/
    3 x 9in
raffia
scissors
10cm/4in florist's
    dry foam ring
stub (floral) wires
reindeer moss
20 dried roses
glue

Spice Decoration

CINNAMON STICKS KEEP THEIR RICH, SPICY SMELL for many years, and provide a perfect base on which to mount other natural decorations. Use any combination of ribbons, lace, gold cord and bells, cones, grasses and seed pods.

YOU WILL NEED

long cinnamon sticks
glue gun
selection of bark, cones, seed
  pods and dried foliage
narrow red ribbon
gold cord and small bell

1 Join the cinnamon sticks together to make a staggered raft shape. Use the glue gun to make this base.

2 Stick individual natural decorations on to the base with dabs of glue from the glue gun.

3 Wrap the ribbon around the bundle, crossing it over several times before tying it at the back. Wind the gold cord around the decoration, tie the bell to the end of the cord, and leave the end with the bell hanging down.

Golden Place Cards

TOUCHES OF GOLD WILL TURN ordinary small, round-cornered cards available from stationery stores into seasonal place cards. If gold doesn't fit into your design scheme, you can create equally lavish place cards with silver paint and pens. Gilded sprigs of fresh rosemary or pine would release a delightful seasonal scent. In addition to designating places at the table, these graceful cards can be used to label foods at a buffet dinner.

1 Score across the midway point of the card using a ruler and craft knife and fold it. Write the guest's name on the front in gold, and add a stick-on jewel, if desired.

2 Paint the leaves on the stems of foliage with gold paint. For a mottled, aged effect, lift off some of the excess paint with a dry sponge. Allow to dry.

3 Use the gilded foliage stem to decorate the card. (Remember, when working with gold, less is more. For an elegant place card, use gold sparingly.) After positioning, attach with glue. Dry flat.

YOU WILL NEED

small, round-cornered cards

ruler

craft knife

cutting mat

gold pen

stick-on jewels (optional)

gold paint

small artist's brush

stems of foliage

soft sponge

all-purpose glue

GILDED NUTS

NUTS ARE IDEAL FOR GILDING, because they have so much texture and detail and can be put to all sorts of decorative uses. They will add glitter and sparkle to sumptuous table decorations for the Christmas feast or look lovely attached in small clusters to gift boxes. Fill a few crystal bowls with gilded nuts and place them around the house to lend a feeling of seasonal splendour. Remember, when using any paints or varnishes, it is essential to keep your work area well ventilated. Work outside, if possible.

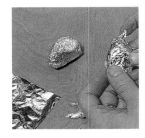

3 Wrap each sized nut in a sheet of Dutch gold metal leaf. Make sure that the nuts are completely covered, with no recesses or details exposed. Don't worry if it looks messy at this point; burnishing will smooth it out.

4 Burnish with a burnishing brush or soft cloth to remove the excess leaf. Seal with a thin, even coat of amber shellac varnish and leave to dry for 30 minutes to 1 hour. Handle carefully as the gold covering is very delicate.

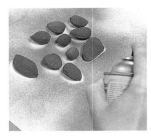

1 Cover a wide, well-ventilated area with old newspaper or thick brown paper. Spray the nuts with red oxide primer. Be sure to coat them well. Leave to dry for 30 minutes to 1 hour.

2 Paint a thin, even coat of water-based size on to each of the nuts, taking care to cover the ridges and recesses. Wait for 20–30 minutes, until the coating becomes clear and tacky.

YOU WILL NEED
assorted nuts
red oxide spray primer
water-based size
1cm/½in paintbrushes
Dutch gold metal leaf
burnishing brush or soft cloth
amber shellac varnish

CHRISTMAS CRACKERS

YOU WILL NEED

double-sided crêpe paper
craft knife and metal ruler
cutting mat
double-sided adhesive tape
**thin card (card stock) in
    white and black**
gold crêpe paper
gold paper-backed foil
corrugated cardboard
fine gold cord
cracker snaps
paper hats, jokes and gifts
narrow black ribbon

1   For each cracker, cut two
25 x 20cm/10 x 8in rectangles of crêpe
paper. Join, overlapping the ends, to
make 45 x 20cm/18 x 8in sheets. Cut
three pieces of white card (card stock)
23 x 10cm/9 x 4in. Roll each into a
cylinder. Overlap the ends by 3cm/1¼in.

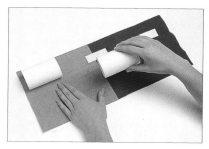

2   Lay strips of double-sided adhesive
tape across the crêpe paper on which to
attach the card cylinders: one in the
centre and the other two about
4cm/1½in in from each end of the
rectangle. Roll up and secure the edge
with double-sided tape.

3   Decorate the cracker with strips of
the gold paper. Lay a strip of paper-
backed foil over a piece of corrugated
cardboard and ease the foil into the
ridges. Cut a star shape out of thin
black cardboard, wrap fine gold cord
around it and stick it on the cracker.

4   Insert a cracker snap and place the
novelties in the central section of the
cracker. Tie up the ends with narrow
ribbon, easing the crêpe paper gently so
that you can tie the knots very tightly.

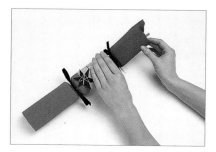

5   Complete the cracker by folding the
edges of the crêpe paper over the ends
of the cardboard tubes.

GLITTERING CONES

THE INTRICATE SHAPE of these cones looks wonderful when highlighted with gold and sliver paint and glitter.

YOU WILL NEED

pine cones
red oxide spray primer
spray paints in gold and
 silver
glue gun or all-purpose glue
 and an old fine
 paintbrush
assorted glitters
saucer
ribbon

1 To provide a good base colour for the spray paint, spray the cones with red oxide primer. Ensure that all the recesses and details are well covered. Leave to dry for 1–2 hours.

2 Spray the cones several times with gold or silver spray. Hold the can 25–30cm/10–12in away from the cones as you spray, taking care to cover the whole cone. Leave to dry.

3 Heat up the glue gun and apply a little glue to the tips of each cone. Take care not to apply too much. Alternatively, apply small dabs of glue on to the cone tips with an old fine paintbrush.

4 Working quickly, sprinkle glitter on to the cones so that it sticks to the glued tips. Use a saucer to catch the excess glitter. To complete the decoration, glue a length of ribbon to the base of each cone for hanging.

Precious Shells

Nature's intricate decoration is often hard to beat, but at Christmas time we can enhance it with subtle gilding. These charming shells can either be hung individually or strung together to form a garland.

You Will Need

shells
blue emulsion (latex) paint
two decorator's paintbrushes
  each 1cm/½in wide
water-based gold size

Dutch metal leaf in
  aluminium or gold on
  transfer paper
pale shellac varnish
strong glue
ribbon

1 Paint each shell with two coats of blue paint. Allow to dry. Paint size on to the shells, smoothing out any air bubbles with the brush. Leave to dry until the size becomes clear.

2 Press the metal leaf on to the shells and use a brush to remove any excess. Varnish and leave to dry. Dab glue on to the tip of each shell and attach a ribbon for hanging.

GILDED DETAILS

ONE OF THE QUICKEST AND EASIEST WAYS to create a gilded Christmas ornament is with gold or silver spray paint. Here are some simple ideas.

Glue nuts together in clusters, either keeping the same variety together or mixing interesting shaped nuts. When the glue has set firm, push a stub (floral) wire through a gap between the nuts, twist it to make a loop and tie on a decorative ribbon or bow.

Be bold in your choice of subjects to spray: dried mushrooms or toadstools are an unusual choice. Dry the fungi in an airing cupboard or an oven at the lowest setting with the door slightly open. After spraying, tie them singly, in pairs or in groups with colourful ribbons.

Store-bought or homemade cookies in fun shapes can be sprayed gold, and they make wonderful subjects for the enthusiastic gilder. You can buy edible gold spray from specialist cake decorating suppliers.

Fruit of all shapes and sizes – pears in particular – look opulent when spatter-sprayed with gold or silver paint. Attach a hook to each stalk and tie on a shiny bow to attach to the tree.

Appliquéd Stars

MIX AND MATCH these festive-coloured felt stars for a bold Christmas display.

1 Using the template at the back of the book, cut out an equal number of red and green stars. Pierce some of the red stars 5mm/¼in from the edge. Cut out smaller stars, leaving a 5mm/¼in border all around.

2 Stitch a red border to one of the green stars with small, even running stitches. Centre a small, red star on a green star and sew 5mm/¼in from the edge again using small, neat running stitches.

3 Place these stars together, sandwiching a plain red star in the middle. Stitch the three stars together at the inner points. Sew a loop of ribbon to one of the points.

4 For a variation, cut a small circle in the centre of a green star. Place a piece of patterned fabric and a red star behind it. Stitch around the hole. Sew the edges of the stars together.

Heraldic Hangings

THESE STYLISH SALT DOUGH decorations look good enough to eat but are purely ornamental.

YOU WILL NEED

2 cups flour
1 cup salt
1 cup tepid water
baking parchment
tracing paper and pencil
scissors and sharp knife
boiled sweets (hard candies)
cocktail stick (toothpick)
acrylic gesso
gold craft paint and brushes
water-based satin varnish
jewels or sequins (optional)
glue (optional)
fine gold cord

Jewels, sequins and painted patterns enhance classic shapes such as fleur-de-lys and stars.

1 Mix flour, salt and water to a firm dough. Knead for 10 minutes. Roll the dough out flat on baking parchment to a thickness of 5mm/¼in. Trace the templates at the back of the book and cut out of the dough. Dust with flour and place a sweet (hard candy) in the centre. Cut around the sweet, adding a 3mm/⅛in margin.

2 Make a hole for hanging in the top of each shape with a cocktail stick (toothpick). Transfer the ornaments, without the sweets, on the paper to a baking sheet and bake at 120°C/ 250°F/Gas ½ for 9 hours. Place a boiled sweet in each hole and return to the oven for 30 minutes. Remove from the oven and set aside to cool.

3 Paint the shapes with gesso and allow to dry. Then paint them with gold paint and allow to dry overnight. Apply five coats of varnish, leaving to dry between applications. Jewels or sequins can also be added at this stage by gluing them on to the surface. Hang the ornaments from gold cord through the top hole.

INDIAN-STYLE DECORATIONS

THESE BRIGHT SALT DOUGH ornaments evoke the vivid colours of an Indian festival.

YOU WILL NEED

2 cups flour
1 cup salt
1 cup tepid water
baking parchment
tracing paper and pencil
thin card (card stock)
scissors and sharp knife
cocktail stick (toothpick)
paintbrushes
acrylic gesso
paints in bright colours
strong glue
selection of beads and
    sequins
matt acrylic varnish
thin ribbon

1 Mix the flour, salt and half the water, then gradually add more water. Knead for 10 minutes. Roll out the dough on baking parchment. Trace the templates from the back of the book and cut out of the dough.

2 Dust the dough with flour. Make the patterns and detail in the dough using the point of a knife or a cocktail stick. Make a hole in the top of each shape for hanging. Moisten the ornaments.

3 Make smaller templates for the relief designs. Cut out of dough and stick them to the shapes. Place on a baking sheet and bake at 120°C/250°F/Gas ½ for 5 hours. Cool.

4 Prime with acrylic gesso. Leave to dry, then paint in bright colours. Glue on beads or sequins. Coat with acrylic varnish when dry. Thread the ribbon through the hole to hang.

CROSS-STITCH CHRISTMAS TREE DECORATION

THIS BRIGHT SEASONAL DESIGN OF HOLLY AND BERRIES will continue to give pleasure for many Christmases to come.

YOU WILL NEED

14 hpi white aida, 13cm/5in square
tapestry needle
stranded embroidery thread (floss) as listed in key
pencil
tape measure
scissors
sewing needle
matching sewing thread
8cm/3¼in embroidery frame (hoop)
felt

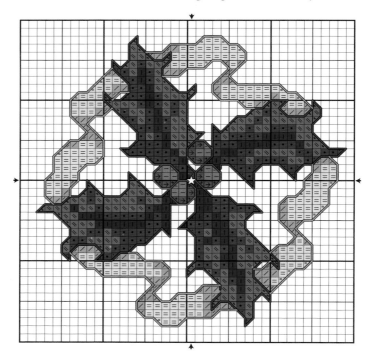

1 Work the design using two strands of thread (floss) for the cross-stitch and one strand for the backstitch.

2 When complete, draw a 10cm/4in circle around the design and cut it out. Work a running stitch 5mm/¼in inside the raw edge. Centre the design over the inside rim of the embroidery frame (hoop) and gather up the thread.

3 Lace the embroidery into the back of the frame and replace the outside ring over the frame. Finish by slip stitching a circle of felt over the back.

Cross stitch in two strands

Dark grass green
Mid grass green
Privet green
Dark red
Berry red
Gold
Deep yellow

Back stitch in one strand

— Mid grass green
— Dark red
— Gold

☆ Middle point

HANGING JUGGLERS

THIS INVENTIVE DECORATION is made from a wire coathanger and small pieces of polymer clay.

YOU WILL NEED

pliers and wire coathanger
gold aerosol paint
epoxy resin glue
¼ block polymer clay
earring wires with loops
modelling tools
sandpaper and thick needle
acrylic paints and brushes
varnish and nylon fishing
line
shell-shaped jewellery
findings
gold cord for hanging

1 Cut the hook and twisted section off the hanger. Twist half the remaining wire into a double-diamond-shaped frame. Spray with gold paint, then glue the wires where they cross.

2 Mould four thumbnail-sized pieces of clay into egg shapes for the heads of the figures. Trim an earring wire, form a hook in the end and embed into each head.

3 Roll small pieces of clay for the limbs and an oblong for each torso. Assemble the bodies and smooth any seams with sandpaper. Cut five stars, two a little larger. Roll five bead shapes and pierce. Bake, as instructed.

4 Paint the figures, beads and stars, then varnish. Assemble the figures and stars on the frame using fishing line and findings. Tie cord to the top for hanging, then glue the large stars on each side, sandwiching the wire.

Velvet Stocking

THIS SUMPTUOUS STOCKING is perfect for holding tiny treats.

1 Enlarge the template for the cuff to the size required and cut out. Pin to a double thickness of gold satin and draw around it with tailor's chalk, leaving a seam allowance. Cut out the pieces.

2 Enlarge the stocking template and divide into three sections. Pin each piece to a double thickness of each colour velvet. Draw around each piece, leaving a seam allowance, and cut out.

3 Pin the three stocking sections together. Then machine stitch the stocking and the gold satin cuff together to make each side of the stocking. On the right side of each piece, pin a strip of decorative braid and sequin ribbon. Sew these on invisibly by hand.

4 With right sides together, stitch the stocking sides and cuff together. Turn through, then fold the satin inside the stocking, leaving a deep cuff. Turn in the raw edge of the cuff, and slip stitch it to the stocking seams. Trim with gold buttons. Attach a loop of braid.

PAINTED STAR CANDLE HOLDER

THE GENTLE GLOW OF CANDLES has an obvious affinity with starlight, and this 12-pointed star is gilded and studded with copper to reflect light. Painted in warm, festive colours, this holder would make a lovely addition to a traditional Christmas table.

1 Using a pair of compasses (a compass), draw a large circle on the plywood. With the same radius, mark the six points of the star around the circle and join with a ruler and pen. Draw a smaller circle on the pine and mark out the second star in the same way. Draw a circle in the centre to fit your chosen candle size.

2 Cut out the two stars and sand any rough edges. Stick together carefully with wood glue to form a 12-pointed star.

3 Paint with white undercoat and sand lightly when dry. Cover with a base coat of dark green acrylic paint, then paint on the design. Seal with a coat of matt varnish.

4 Using the bradawl, make six holes for the copper disk rivets. Trim the stems of the rivets with wire cutters and push into the holes.

YOU WILL NEED

pair of compasses
5mm/¼in birch plywood sheet
ruler
pen
1cm/½in pine
fretsaw
sandpaper
wood glue

paintbrushes
white undercoat
acrylic paints in green, red, gold
matt varnish
bradawl
six 2cm/¾in copper disc rivets
wire cutters

Printed Star Wrapping Paper

COMPLETE AN ORIGINAL GIFT by dressing it up with original, hand-decorated wrapping paper that's not only stylish but fun to make. This star pattern printed in festive colours makes great Christmas wrapping. Silver on blue is also an elegant combination. Stamp matching gift tags too, if you wish.

YOU WILL NEED

thin cardboard for template

scissors

chalk

plain sheet of wrapping paper, preferably a matt craft paper

star-shaped rubber stamp, in one or more sizes

red, green, white and gold acrylic paints

artist's brush

1 Cut a cardboard circle. Trace around the template with chalk on to the wrapping paper. Space the circles evenly on the sheet.

2 Print the perimeters of alternate circles with red and green stars, brushing the paint evenly on to the stamp between each print.

3 Print white stars in the middle of each chalk circle, between the circles and in each corner of the wrapping paper.

4 Following the chalk circle between the stars, make rings of gold dots and dot the point of each star with gold.

Natural Gift Wraps

EVEN THE MOST BASIC BROWN WRAPPING PAPER can take on a very special look. Use a gilded skeletonized leaf and gold twine in combination with brown paper. Coarser string gives a more robust look.

FILIGREE LEAF WRAP

This beautiful wrap is a clear case of lily-gilding.

1 Rub wax gilt into the skeletonized leaf.

2 Wrap a gift in brown paper and rub wax gilt on to the corners.

3 Tie the package with gold twine, bringing the ends together and making a knot. Fray the ends to create a tassel effect. Slip the leaf under the twine, securing it with glue at each end if necessary. The leaves are delicate, so keep the gift clear of other packages once under the tree.

FRUIT AND FOLIAGE WRAP

Here, gilded brown paper provides a fitting background for a decoration of leaves and dried fruit.

1 Wrap the package with brown paper and rub in wax gilt, paying special attention to the corners.

2 Tie the parcel with seagrass string, then glue a different dried fruit or leaf to each quarter.

YOU WILL NEED

picture framer's wax gilt	glue gun or all-purpose glue
large skeletonized leaf	seagrass string
brown paper	dried fruit slices, such as apples and oranges
tape	
gold twine	preserved leaves

Ice Box

A GREAT BIG BOX UNDER THE CHRISTMAS TREE always attracts attention. Plain blue paper is stencilled with snowflakes, then the whole gift is bunched up in clear, ice-like cellophane.

YOU WILL NEED

tracing paper and pencil

thin card (card stock) or
    acetate sheet

craft knife

cutting mat

bright blue wrapping paper

small sponge

white watercolour paint

clear adhesive tape

scissors

roll of clear, wide cellophane

silver foil ribbon

selection of silver
    Christmas tree ornaments

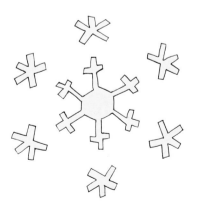

1 Enlarge the snowflake design as required, trace it and transfer it to the card (card stock) or acetate sheet. Cut out the stencil carefully, using a craft knife and a cutting mat, then place the stencil over the wrapping paper.

2 Use a small damp sponge to apply the white watercolour paint sparingly through the stencil. Stencil the snowflakes randomly all over the blue paper, continuing over the edges. Leave the paper to dry.

3 If necessary, join enough stencilled sheets of wrapping paper with adhesive tape to make one large sheet to wrap the box. Cut a length of cellophane long enough to pass under the box and up the sides, with at least 30cm/12in extra on both ends. Do the same in the other direction, to cross over the first sheet under the box.

4 Gather up the cellophane on top of the boxed gift, making sure that the sides of the box are completely covered. Bunch the ends close to the box top and tape them tightly.

5 Cover the adhesive tape with silver foil ribbon and tie in a bow. Trim the ends of the ribbon and attach the tree ornaments.

Bold Red and Gold Gift Wrap

THERE IS SOMETHING SUMPTUOUS ABOUT RED TISSUE PAPER — the rustling noise and smooth texture impart a sense of luxury, and the colour deepens with layering.

You Will Need

red tissue paper
scrap paper
big star rubber stamp
gold ink
clear adhesive tape
scissors
gold ribbon, cord or tinsel

1 Place red tissue paper on scrap paper. Beginning in one corner, work diagonally across each sheet, stamping gold stars 5cm/2in apart. Leave to dry.

2 Wrap the gift using a lining of two sheets of plain red tissue paper under the stamped sheet. Use clear adhesive tape to secure the ends.

3 Trim the wrapped gift with a gold ribbon, cord or tinsel tied on top in a single bow.

4 To finish, cut the ribbon ends into generous swallowtails to match the points of the gold stars.

Christmas Tree Gift Tags

BEAUTIFUL HAND-MADE GIFT TAGS add the finishing touch to your carefully wrapped presents.

You Will Need

pencil and metal ruler
cellulose kitchen sponge
scissors
glue stick
corrugated cardboard
gold and black stencil paint
coloured and textured paper
tracing paper
thin card (card stock) or
    acetate sheet
craft knife and cutting mat
white cartridge (heavy) paper
paintbrushes
bright watercolour inks
white oil crayon
brown parcel wrap
thin coloured card (card
    stock)
hole punch and metal ruler
fine gold cord

1 Draw the Christmas tree motif on the kitchen sponge and cut out carefully to make a positive and a negative image. Glue each stamp to a piece of cardboard. Stamp both motifs in gold on to a selection of papers in different textures and colours (use tracing paper as well).

3 Paint plain white cartridge (heavy) paper with watercolour ink in bright, vivid colours and then cut simple star motifs from the different colours.

2 Trace the Christmas tree branch pattern and transfer it to a piece of thin cardboard (card stock) or acetate. Cut out using a craft knife. Stencil some branches in black and others in gold on to a selection of different papers and on some of the stamped gold motifs.

4 Use a white oil crayon to scribble spots on brown parcel wrap for snowflakes. Tear them out individually leaving a border of brown paper.

5 Using a craft knife and a metal ruler, cut out tags from thin cardboard in various colours. Cut or tear a selection of motifs, arrange them on the tags and glue down. Punch a hole in the top and thread it with a loop of gold cord.

Winter Heart

A PLUMP, SOFT HEART edged in bold blanket stitch will make an original addition to your tree.

You Will Need

tracing paper and pencil

scissors

scraps of woollen fabrics in two colours

polyester wadding (batting)

pins

embroidery thread (floss)

needle

garden twine

1   Trace the template at the back of the book and cut out two hearts in each fabric. Cut two small strips for the cross. Use the template again to cut out a piece of wadding (batting), then trim off 1cm/⅜in all around the edge.

2   Pin the cross pieces on to the contrasting fabric and attach with large stitches, using three strands of embroidery thread (floss) in a contrasting colour.

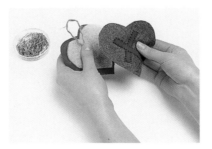

3   Pin all the layers together, sandwiching the wadding between the fabric hearts. Make a loop of twine for hanging the ornament and insert the ends in the top.

4   Sew all around the edges of the heart in blanket stitch using three strands of embroidery thread. Make sure the hanging loop is secured with the stitches.

TREE ORNAMENTS

THE CHRISTMAS TREE IS THE CENTREPIECE OF SEASONAL DECORATING. MAKE IT SPECIAL WITH BEAUTIFUL, HANDMADE ORNAMENTS.

Heavenly Gold Star

Collect as many types of gold paper as you can find to cover this sparkling star, with its subtle variations of texture. It makes an attractive wall or mantelpiece decoration, and it would look equally splendid at the top of the tree. Try this technique on other shapes as well – to make a gilded sphere or cone, for instance.

1   Tear different types of gold paper into scraps of different sizes. Try to make a good assortment.

2   Dilute PVA (white) glue with a little water. Paint it on to the back of a piece of gold paper and stick it to the star.

3   Paint some more glue over the scrap of paper to secure it to the star. Work all over the front of the star, using different papers to vary the texture and colour. Make a loop of wire and stick the ends into the back of the star for hanging. Secure with masking tape.

4   Cover the back of the star with different kinds of gold paper.

5   Leave the glue to dry thoroughly, then cover the star with a coat of gold glitter paint.

YOU WILL NEED

assorted gold papers such as sweet (candy) wrappers, metallic crêpe paper or giftwrap

PVA (white) glue

paintbrushes

polystyrene (styrofoam) star

fine wire

masking tape

gold glitter paint

Exotic Ornaments

THESE SEQUINNED AND BEADED BALLS look like a collection of priceless Fabergé treasures, yet they're simple and fun to make. Hang them on the tree or pile them in a dish for a show-stopping decoration.

1 Make a template by cutting a paper circle large enough to cover the ball completely. Pin the netting to the template and cut it out. If desired, cut lengths of gold braid and pin around the ball to make a framework for your sequins.

2 Secure the netting to the ball using tiny pieces of tape. Don't worry if it looks a little messy; the tape and raw edges will be hidden later with sequins.

3 Attach a loop of gold braid to the ball with a brass-headed pin.

4 Thread a bead and sequin on to a brass-headed pin and gently press into the ball. Repeat until you have the number of designs required.

TIP

When working out your designs use simple, repeating patterns and avoid using too many colours at a time.

YOU WILL NEED

silk-covered
  decorative balls
paper for
  template
scissors
pins
gold netting
gold braid

tape
brass-headed pins,
  1cm/½in long
small glass and
  pearl beads
sequins in a
  variety of shapes
  and colours

ℛaffia ℬalls

To give your Christmas tree a natural look, these raffia balls have a subtle shade and interesting texture.

You Will Need

scissors
small polystyrene (styrofoam)
   balls
double-sided adhesive tape
natural (garden) raffia

Tip

Vary the basic design by using coloured raffia, or glue some dried flowers or cones to the top of the balls.

1   Make a short piece of wire into a loop. Push the ends into a polystyrene (styrofoam) ball.

2   Cover the ball completely in double-sided adhesive tape to form a base for the raffia.

3   Arrange the hank of raffia so that you can remove lengths without tangling them. Holding the first 10cm/4in of the strand at the top of the ball, wind the raffia around, working from top to bottom and covering the shape as evenly as possible.

4   When you have finished covering the ball, tie the end of the raffia to the length you left free at the beginning. Using a few strands of raffia together, tie a bow over these two ends to finish off the top of the decoration.

Gilded Glass Spheres

With a gold glass-painting outliner, you can turn plain glass tree decorations into unique gilded ornaments. Simple repeating motifs such as circles, triangles and stars are most effective.

You Will Need

plain glass tree ornaments
detergent
white spirit (paint thinner)
soft cloth
gold glass-painting outliner
paper tissues
jam jar
wire-edged ribbon

1 Before you begin to apply the paint, clean the glass thoroughly with detergent and wipe it with white spirit (paint thinner) to remove grease.

2 Working on one side only, gently squeeze the gold glass-painting outliner on to the glass. If you make a mistake, wipe it off quickly with a paper tissue while it is still wet.

3 Rest the sphere on an empty jar and leave for about 24 hours to dry. Decorate the other side.

4 Thread a length of wire-edged ribbon through the loop at the top of the ornament and tie it in a bow.

$\mathscr{S}$HINY $\mathscr{S}$NOWFLAKES

THESE SPARKLING DECORATIONS are easy to make by simply cutting patterns out of shiny reflective papers. A mixture of gold, silver and coloured papers will reflect the tree lights perfectly.

YOU WILL NEED

pencil
pair of compasses (compass)
reflective papers in gold,
    silver and several colours
scissors
tracing paper
craft knife
cutting mat
gold thread

1 Draw a circle on the back of the reflective paper and cut it out. Fold the circle in half three times. Photocopy the patterns from the back of the book, enlarging them if necessary.

2 Trace one of the geometric designs on to a pattern and transfer it on to the folded shiny paper circle. Use a sharp pencil, as the detail is intricate and must be precise.

3 Cut out the traced pattern shapes, using a craft knife to make small, internal cuts. Unfold the circle and flatten. Do the same with the other papers and geometric patterns.

4 For the curved pattern, unfold once and fold in half the other way, then cut out triangular notches along the fold line. Attach lengths of gold thread to hang the snowflakes.

Sequinned Balls

SEQUINS MAKE WONDERFUL Christmas tree decorations, twinkling and sparkling in the light. You can follow this design or create your own patterns.

You Will Need

marker pen

compressed cotton or polystyrene (styrofoam) balls

concave sequins in a variety of colours and shapes

lill (straight) pins

beading thread and needle

small bronze-coloured glass beads

fluted metal beads

dressmaker's pins

1 Use a marker pen to divide each polystyrene (styrofoam) ball into quarters. Mark around the middle of the ball to divide it into eight sections.

2 Outline the sections with sequins in different colours, attaching them with lill (straight) pins. Overlap the sequins slightly so that the ball does not show through.

3 Fill in each section with sequins, again overlapping the sequins slightly to hide the ball. You may want to make each section a different colour, or combine colours.

4 Make a loop for hanging and thread small bronze-coloured beads on to it. Thread a metal bead on to a dressmaker's pin and press into the ball to secure the loop.

Ribbon Ornaments

A WELCOME CHANGE from store-bought decorations, these stylish designs make use of the many attractive ribbons now available. Silk ribbon is the most appealing as it will catch the light.

YOU WILL NEED

FOR THE RIBBON BALL
polystyrene (styrofoam) ball
assortment of plain ribbons
patterned ribbon
dressmaker's pins
scissors
gold lace pins
small gold beads
gold coin pendants
large, ornate gold bead

FOR THE CONE PARCEL
narrow ribbon
pine cone
wide ribbon or ready-made
  bow
all-purpose glue

FOR THE GOLDEN TASSEL
small compressed cotton or
  polystyrene (styrofoam)
  ball
needle and scissors
gold ribbon
all-purpose glue

RIBBON BALL

1 Cover the ball with a variety of ribbons, securing each with pins. Decorate the ball with gold beads and coin pendants using lace pins.

GOLDEN TASSEL

1 Make a hole through the ball and insert lengths of ribbon. Dab glue on to the ball, then fold down the ribbons until the ball is covered.

CONE PARCEL

1 Wrap narrow ribbon around the cone as if wrapping a parcel. Tie a bow at the top and dab with glue to secure. Make a ribbon loop to hang.

2 Wrap a ribbon around the base. To make a loop, thread the needle with a ribbon and insert through the hole in the ball. Knot the ends and trim.

Gilded Stars

HANG THESE FESTIVE STARS on different lengths of ribbon for a sparkling effect.

YOU WILL NEED

15cm/6in squares of medium density fibreboard (MDF) and protective face mask

coping saw or fretsaw

sandpaper

electric or hand drill

red oxide spray primer

water-based size

2.5cm/1in wide paintbrush

Dutch metal leaf in gold and aluminium

burnishing brush

steel wool

methylated spirit (turpentine)

shellac varnish

acrylic varnishing wax

green and blue acrylic paint

dome-shaped plastic jewels

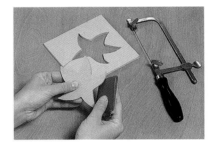

1 Trace the template from the back of the book and transfer it on to MDF. Cut out stars with a saw, sandpaper the edges and drill a hole at the top. Spray both sides with primer.

2 Paint on a thin, even coat of size and leave for 20-30 minutes. Gild each star with gold or aluminium metal leaf, then burnish with a burnishing brush or soft cloth.

3 Dip some steel wool into a little methylated spirit (turpentine) and gently rub the edges of each star. Paint a thin, even coat of shellac varnish over the gold leaf and varnishing wax over the aluminium leaf.

4 Mix the green and blue paints with a little water. Paint each star, leave for 5 minutes, then remove most of the paint with a cloth. Glue a plastic jewel in the centre. Tie a piece of ribbon through each hole for hanging.

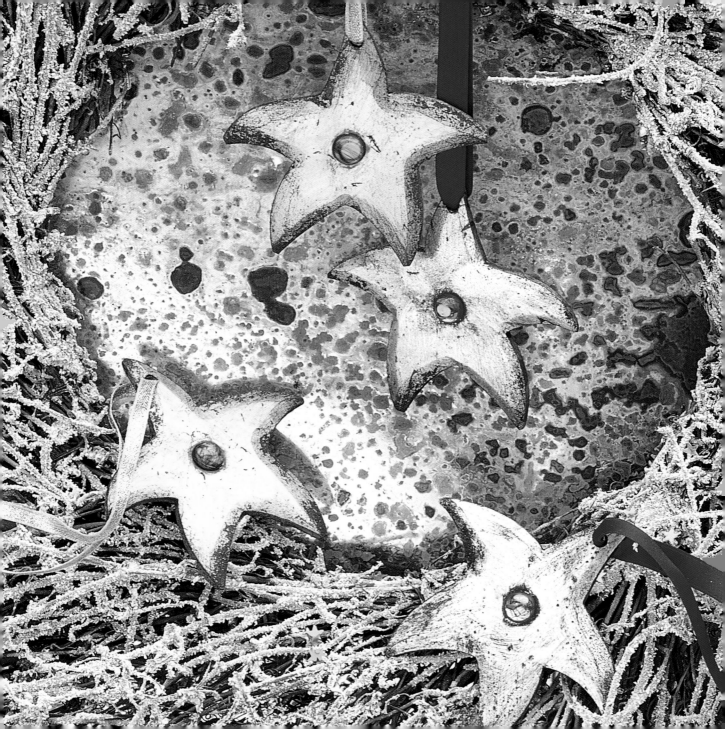

Papier-Mache Decorations

THESE COLOURFUL ORNAMENTS are easy to make from scraps of newspaper.

YOU WILL NEED
tracing paper
pencil
thin cardboard
craft knife
cutting mat
small metal jewellery findings
strong clear glue
newspaper
diluted PVA (white) glue
container for glue
artist's paintbrushes
white paint
poster paints
paint-mixing palette
clear gloss varnish
thin cord

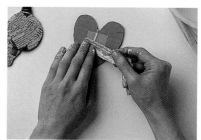

1 Cut cardboard templates from the back of the book and glue a jewellery finding on to the back of each ornament. Allow to dry, then cover with three layers of thin newspaper strips soaked in diluted PVA glue. Dry overnight and prime with a coat of white paint. Leave to dry.

2 Draw your design, then paint with poster paints. Seal with a coat of varnish and suspend with thin cord.

Silk Purse Tree Ornaments

RIBBONS ARE AVAILABLE IN A GREAT RANGE OF widths and colours, and you need only a small amount of each to make these delicate little purses. Use contrasting shades for generous bows around the top.

YOU WILL NEED

an assortment
   of pretty ribbons
scissors
pins
matching thread
needle
fine gold cord
polyester wadding
   (batting)

1 Cut strips of ribbon long enough to make a purse when folded in the middle, allowing for the raw edges to be folded down at the top. To make a striped purse, pin, then stitch narrower lengths of ribbon together with running stitch.

2 With right sides together, sew up the sides of the purse.

3 Turn right side out and tuck in the raw edges. Stitch on a loop of fine gold cord and stuff lightly with wadding (batting).

4 Gather the top of the purse and tie with another piece of ribbon, finishing with a colourful bow.

Embroidered Dragonflies

These delicate iridescent insects make original decorations for your tree.

You Will Need

tracing paper
pencil
black marker pen
water-soluble fabric
opalescent cellophane
small pieces of sheer
  synthetic organdie in
  brown and green
dressmaker's pins
embroidery frame
sewing machine with fine
  needle
metallic thread in two
  thicknesses
spray varnish
scissors
glittery pipecleaners
sewing needle
small glass beads
fine wire
all-purpose glue

1 Trace the templates on to soluble fabric. Put the cellophane between two pieces of organdie and pin under the frame. Stitch around the wings in straight stitch using metallic thread.

2 Using fine metallic thread in the needle and thick thread in the bobbin, machine stitch the outlines in straight stitch. Fill in the shapes. Remove the hoop and dissolve the fabric in water.

3 Varnish the insects and leave to dry. Cut a pipecleaner longer than each body and sew to the underside as far as the head. Trim and bend the rest of the embroidery under the head and body to cover the pipecleaner.

4 Fold the wings into a raised position and stitch. Thread glass beads on to the wire, twist into antennae and attach to the head. Glue the insects directly to the branches of the tree.

Elegant Tassels

THESE DELICATE TASSELS make stunning Christmas ornaments suspended from the branches of the tree.

You Will Need

scissors
silk or metallic embroidery
   thread (floss)
thin polyester thread
cord
comb
fine twine

1 Cut and fold lengths of embroidery threads (floss) and place them on top of the polyester thread. Loop a length of cord, knot the ends and place on the embroidery threads. Tie the polyester thread tightly around the cord.

2 Cut through the folded ends of the embroidery threads, then comb out the tassel. Make a small loop with the fine twine.

Tassels look especially splendid when gilded. These tassels have been coated with red oxide primer, left to dry and then sprayed with three applications of gold spray paint. The fronds of the tassels may form clumps which can be separated with a comb before they dry.

3 Working from top to bottom of the ball of the tassel, neatly bind the twine tightly around the top of the tassel as shown. Pass the end of the twine through the loop.

4 Pull the twine up into the binding and snip off the ends. Make a loop in a strand of the cord and pass the cord through the loop. Trim the cut ends of the tassel and hang from the cord.

FESTIVE FIGURES

POLYMER CLAY IS PERFECT for making Christmas ornaments – it is easy to use and extremely versatile.

YOU WILL NEED

roller

polymer clay in various colours

Christmas pastry (cookie) cutters

modelling tool

fine paintbrush

plastic straw

bronze powders in various colours

varnish

glue

rhinestones

cocktail stick (toothpick)

narrow ribbon

1 Roll out the clay to a thickness of 1cm/½in and press out the shapes using pastry (cookie) cutters. Cut a good selection of figures and sizes.

2 Draw markings with a modelling tool and make small indentations for the rhinestones on the reindeer with the blunt end of a paintbrush.

3 Make a hanging hole in the top centre with a straw. Brush on different coloured bronze powders and blend together. Bake following the manufacturer's instructions.

4 Apply a coat of varnish and leave to dry. Glue rhinestones in the indentations, using a cocktail stick (toothpick). Thread a length of ribbon through the hole for hanging.

Edible Ornaments

These tasty decorations will delight children and adults. This recipe makes about twelve ornaments.

You Will Need

baking parchment
175g/6oz/½ cup plain
    flour
75g/3oz/5 tbsp butter
40g/1½oz/3 tbsp caster
    (superfine) sugar
egg white
30ml/2 tbsp orange juice
pastry (cookie) cutter
round 1cm/½in pastry
    (cookie) cutter
225g/8oz coloured fruit
    sweets (candies)
coloured ribbons

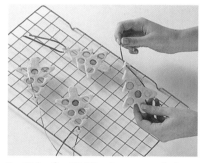

1 Preheat the oven to 180°C/350°F/ Gas 4. Line a baking sheet with baking parchment. Sift the flour into a mixing bowl. Cut the butter into pieces and rub into the flour until it resembles breadcrumbs. Stir in the sugar, egg white and enough orange juice to form a soft dough. Knead on a lightly floured surface until smooth.

2 Roll out thinly and stamp out as many shapes as possible using a Christmas tree cutter. Transfer the shapes to the lined baking sheet, spaced well apart. Using a round cutter, stamp out six circles from each tree. Cut each sweet (candy) into three slices and place a piece in each hole. Make a small hole at the top of each tree.

3 Bake for 15-20 minutes, until the trees are golden and the sweets have melted, filling the holes. Cool on the baking sheets for 5 minutes and then transfer to a wire rack to cool. Thread lengths of ribbon through the holes at the top for hanging. Store in an airtight container until ready to hang.

Beaded Finials

THESE DELICATE CREATIONS, enhanced with pendant beads, started life as the cardboard backing on envelopes.

You Will Need

tracing paper and pencil
medium-weight manila
    cardboard (card stock)
scissors
craft knife and metal ruler
cutting mat
bradawl (awl)
beads
flat-headed pins
long-nosed pliers
thin cord

1   Trace the templates from the back of the book. Transfer to card (card stock) twice and cut out. Mark the slotting slits down the centre of both pieces and cut out using a craft knife, metal ruler and cutting mat.

2   Make six small holes with a bradawl (awl): one close to the bottom edge of one piece and one on the outside edge of the four top curls for inserting the beads, and a hole at the top for the hanging loop.

3   Thread the beads on to the pins. Bend each pin close to the top of the beads with pliers. Then hook the pins through the card. Wrap the ends around the pin, to secure.

4   After firmly slotting the two beaded card pieces together, thread a piece of cord through the top hole. Tie the ends to make a loop for hanging.

$\mathscr{S}$PARKLING $\mathscr{S}$TARS

SHIMMERING SEQUINS and tiny beads make these hanging stars really shine.

YOU WILL NEED

polystyrene (styrofoam) star
with hanging loop
gold spray paint
small piece of modelling
clay
brown paper
glass seed beads
multi-coloured sequins
seed pearl beads
special-design sequins
1.5cm/⅝in brass-headed
pins
thin gold braid
scissors

1 Spray the star with gold paint, anchoring it with a piece of modelling clay to a sheet of brown paper to stop it moving. Allow to dry.

2 While the star is drying, sort the beads, sequins and pins into containers to make it easier to choose colours and shapes as you work.

3 Thread a glass seed bead on to a pin, followed by a multi-coloured sequin. Push it gently into the star. Repeat to complete the design, covering the whole star. Pin a seed pearl bead and special-design sequin in the centre of each side of the star.

4 For an alternative design, decorate the edges of the star with lines of sequins in contrasting colours. Pick out the "bones" of the star, in the same way, leaving the inner sections gold. Attach a length of gold braid through the loop to hang the star.

Wire Angel

This elegant Christmas angel will grace the top of your tree year after year.

YOU WILL NEED

silver- or gold-plated wire,
   1mm/0.039in thick
round-nosed pliers
parallel pliers
wire cutters
narrow ribbon
silver or gold star

1 Use the template at the back of the book as a guide. Leaving 5cm/2in at the end, begin to bend the wire around the template. Use round-nosed pliers for the larger curls and parallel pliers for the more delicate curls.

2 Continue bending the wire into the angel shape. When you reach the waist, bend the wire across to form the waistband. Make a series of seven long horizontal loops with curled ends back along the waistband.

3 When you reach the final curls of the shoulder, loop the wire around the back of the shoulder and under the bottom of the wing. Finish off with a coil, then cut off the wire.

4 Using the wire left at the start, bind the shoulder and wing together. Cut off the end. Thread ribbon through the loops in the waistband and hang a star from the hand.

HARLEQUIN EGGS

THESE RICH, METALLIC-EFFECT ORNAMENTS are in fact blown eggs, decorated with gold and silver gilt cream.

Suspend them from the Christmas tree or an alternative such as pussy willow or holly.

YOU WILL NEED

eggs and wire egg-holders
pale blue acrylic paint
paintbrushes and soft cloth
white pencil
gilt cream in gold and silver

Plain gold gilded eggs are also very decorative. They are blown first, then gilded with gilt cream and polished to a shine. A combination of silver and gold eggs, suspended from the branches of a real Christmas tree, will look extremely elegant.

1 Blow the eggs by making a hole at each end and blowing the contents out. Paint half of each egg with pale blue. Leave to dry, then paint the other half in the same colour.

2 Using a white pencil, and with a steady hand, draw horizontal and vertical lines over the egg to make a checked pattern. This pattern can be adjusted to suit your own design.

3 Using a fine paintbrush, paint gold gilt cream in alternate squares, taking care to keep the edges neat. Leave to dry. Paint the silver squares in the same way and leave to dry.

4 Carefully polish the egg with a soft cloth to a high shine. Hold the two prongs of the wire egg-holder firmly together and push them into the hole at the top of the egg for hanging.

GINGERBREAD MEN

MAKE THESE PRETTY DECORATIONS using your favourite gingerbread recipe; they will be popular with all ages.

YOU WILL NEED

two large baking sheets
gingerbread dough
rolling pin
8cm/3¼in gingerbread man
   biscuit (cookie) cutter
skewer
wire rack
royal icing
piping bag, fitted with
   writing nozzle
two bowls
food colouring in green and
   blue
lemon juice
silver dragees
narrow gingham ribbon

There is a wide range of cookie and pastry cutters available on the market. Santas are a traditional family favourite.

1 Preheat the oven to 180°C/ 350°F/Gas 4. Grease the baking sheets. Roll out the gingerbread dough on a floured surface and cut out the gingerbread figures. Space them well apart on the baking sheets.

2 Re-roll the dough trimmings and cut into strips, 1cm/½in wide and 28cm/11in long. Place a strip around each man. Make a hole in the top with a skewer. Bake for 12–15 minutes, then cool on a wire rack.

3 Put icing in the piping bag. Pipe in the details. Divide the remaining icing equally between two bowls. Colour one green and the other blue. Thin the icing with lemon juice.

4 Ice the body of each figure. Add a row of dragee buttons. Leave to set for 2 hours. Decorate the edges and buttons with white icing. Thread the figures with ribbon for hanging.

FRUIT AND FLOWER DECORATIONS

NATURAL DECORATIONS COMPLEMENT an evergreen tree perfectly.

FLORAL STARS AND TREES

1 Cut the block of foam into slices approximately 2.5cm/1in thick. Using the pastry (cookie) cutters, press out star and tree shapes. Put the lavender with two tablespoons of gold dust powder in the plastic bag and shake to mix. Liberally coat all the surfaces of the foam shapes with florist's adhesive.

2 Place the shapes in the plastic bag and shake. As a variation, press dried tulip and rose petals on to the shapes before putting them in the bag; only the exposed glued areas will pick up the lavender. Alternatively, glue a cranberry to the centre of the stars. Make a small hole in each shape, and thread with gold cord for hanging.

DRIED FRUIT DECORATIONS

1 Tie gold cord around the fruit, and knot it on top to form a hanging loop. Stick a rose head to the top next to the knotted cord. Dab glue on to cinnamon sticks and place them next to the rose head.

Rococo Star

PERSUADE THE FAIRY TO TAKE a well-earned rest this year, and make a magnificent gold star to take pride of place at the top of the tree, or hanging from the branches.

YOU WILL NEED

tracing paper and pencil
thin cardboard (card stock)
scissors and newspaper
corrugated cardboard
craft knife and cutting mat
PVA (white) glue
large paintbrush
gold spray paint
gold relief paint
gold glitter

1 Trace the template from the back of the book and transfer it on to cardboard (card stock). Cut out and draw around it on the corrugated cardboard, using a craft knife and cutting mat. Tear the newspaper into small strips and brush watered-down glue on to both sides. Stick the newspaper strips on to the star.

2 Neatly cover the edges and points of the star with the newpaper strips. Allow to dry, then apply a second layer. If the star begins to buckle, place it under a heavy weight. When completely dry, spray both sides with gold paint and leave to dry.

3 Draw a design on one side in gold relief paint and sprinkle with glitter while wet. Allow to dry completely before repeating the design on the other side. If you are hanging the star, attach gold braid from the top point with a dab of glue.

Twiggy Stars

THESE PRETTY STARS WILL LOOK effective either hanging from the branches of the tree or displayed on the top.

You Will Need

secateurs (pruning shears)
willow twigs
stranded embroidery thread (floss)
scissors
checked cotton fabric
natural (garden) raffia (optional)

1 For a large star to top the tree, cut the twigs into lengths of 15cm/6in using the secateurs (pruning shears). For smaller stars to hang from the branches of the tree, cut the twigs into lengths of 5cm/2in. You will need five twigs for each star.

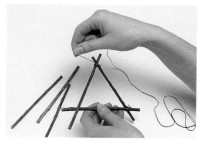

2 Tie the first pair of twigs together near the ends with a length of embroidery thread (floss), winding it around to form a V-shape. Repeat with the remaining twigs, arranging them under and over each other to form a five-pointed star.

3 Cut the checked cotton fabric into thin strips approximately 15 x 2cm/ 6 x ¾in. Leave the ends frayed – this will add to the rustic look.

4 Tie a length of fabric in a double knot over the thread at each point of the star. Attach a loop of raffia if the stars are to be hung.

GLITTERY BALLS

DRESS UP PLAIN GOLD AND SILVER store-bought balls with delicate patterns traced in extra-fine glitter.

YOU WILL NEED

gold and silver contour paste

glass balls and glitter

roll of tape or drinking glass

1 Squeeze contour paste on to each ball in zigzags. Pour glitter over the contour paste, working in sections and allowing each section to dry. Rest the ball on a roll of tape or in a glass while it dries.

2 If you want to add some more intricate detail to the ball, allow all the glitter sections to dry before adding more dabs of contour paste and sprinkling with glitter.

ℬUTTON ℊARLAND

A COLLECTION OF BUTTONS takes on a new life as an unusual garland for the Christmas tree.

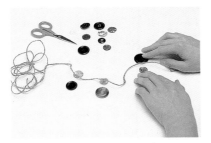

1 Spread all the buttons out so that you can choose a variety of colours and sizes. Balance the weight of the buttons by spacing small ones with larger ones along the garland.

2 Put a small dab of glue on the back of a button. Place the twine on top and wait until the glue hardens before gluing another button on top. Glue the buttons along the twine spacing them evenly. Tie around the tree.

<table>
<tr><td colspan="2">YOU WILL NEED</td></tr>
<tr><td>assortment of buttons in
   various sizes and colours</td><td>glue sticks
garden twine</td></tr>
<tr><td>glue gun</td><td>scissors</td></tr>
</table>

TEMPLATES

THESE TEMPLATES can be scaled up or down on a photocopier as required.

Shiny Snowflakes pp 152–3

Wire Angel pp 174–5

Gilded Stars pp 158–9

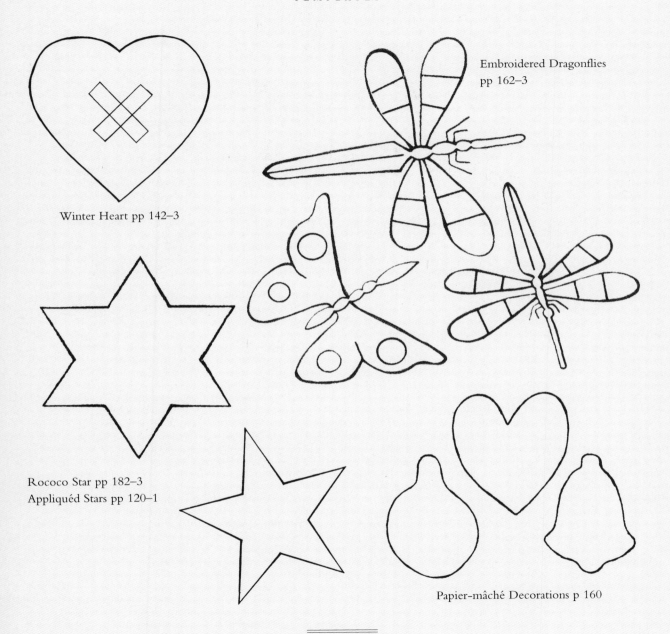

Winter Heart pp 142–3

Embroidered Dragonflies
pp 162–3

Rococo Star pp 182–3
Appliquéd Stars pp 120–1

Papier-mâché Decorations p 160

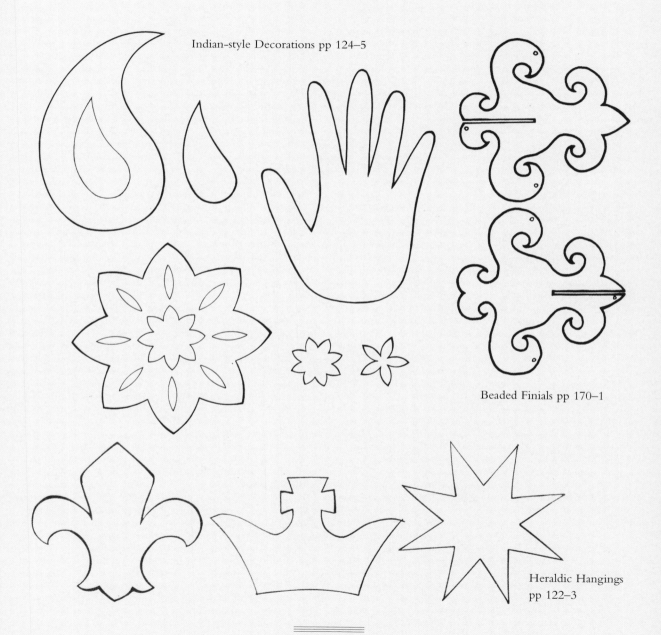

Indian-style Decorations pp 124–5

Beaded Finials pp 170–1

Heraldic Hangings
pp 122–3